Dancing with Voice

Dancing with Voice

A Collaborative Journey across Disciplines

Joan Melton

Voice Theatre Solutions
New York, NY

Cover photo by Karen O'Donnell Photography

ISBN: 1514378213
ISBN 13: 9781514378212
Library of Congress Control Number: 2015909712
CreateSpace Independent Publishing Platform
North Charleston, South Carolina

To

Participants in Exploratory Research Studies

London and Brisbane

Contents

Foreword ···ix

Acknowledgements·····································xi

Introduction··xiii

Part I – Interviews with Dancers ···························1

1   Rusty Curcio – Voice and Dance Techniques·················3

2   William F. Lett - Putting It All Together···················15

3   Francine Zerfas - Dancer to Actor to Voice Specialist···········27

Part II – Research·····································35

4   Ab Prints and the Triple Threat························37

5   Breath Management Strategies across Performance Genres·······45

6   Tucking the Pelvis: Actual and Perceived Outcomes··········53

Part III – Triple Threats on Dancing with Voice · · · · · · · · · · · · · · · · 61

7   Interview with Rin Allen · 63

8   Interview with Mara Davi · 75

9   Interview with John Robert Armstrong · 87

Part IV – Research in Motion · 103

10 Practical Cats & a Laban Approach to Characterization· · · · · · · · 105

11 Widening the Lens· 113

    Bibliography· 115

Foreword

I met Joan Melton over a decade ago at a Voice Foundation Symposium in Philadelphia. I walked into the Theatre at the Academy of Vocal Arts and took my place in a circle of people around her. I remember the first thing she asked us to do was jog in place. She made the simple comment, "Your body will breathe for you." Simple, but it stuck with me.

Not long after that encounter, Joan came to interview me at my studio in New York City for her second book, *Singing in Musical Theatre: The Training of Singers and Actors*. She was on the faculty at Cal State Fullerton at the time and invited me there to work with her students. We began to develop a friendship based on our mutual fascination for the workings of the human voice. She had already begun to envision the path her research would take.

After "retiring" from academia, Joan launched herself into a whirlwind of research and creative activity that has effectively transformed the way voice professionals think about training actors to sing and speak. Her jewel of a book, *One Voice*, now in its second edition, makes a compellingly logical case for integrating voice, movement and singing as inextricably related disciplines.

Dancing with Voice completes the circle. Joan came to visit us at Penn State and spoke about her research on breathing as it relates to all movement, singing included. Her interviews with dancers, dance teachers, and "triple threats" shed light on the unifying aspect of all the disciplines required to train performers, where the developed skill is never an end in itself but a means to communicate a story expressively. Why should breathing for dancing be in conflict with breathing for singing? Or speaking? Isn't breath what fuels all our storytelling? Joan has a real knack for the interview format and elicits surprising insights from her subjects. She writes her own commentary in a clear, personal, accessible and inviting style.

Those of us in the musical theatre trenches know the power of Joan's message in our work with young performers. Rather than operating in isolation, we can take her cue to train collaboratively with shared goals and strategies.

This is Joan Melton's eloquent charge to teachers and performers. The whole is considerably greater than the sum of its parts.

Mary Saunders-Barton
Head of Voice for Musical Theatre
Program Head: MFA in Voice Pedagogy for Musical Theatre
Penn State University
American Academy of Teachers of Singing

Acknowledgements

This book developed over several years. I knew I would write it eventually. But the format and specific content were not clear. The questions were clear, but answers came from multiple directions.

The first director/choreographer I interviewed formally was Rusty Curcio (Chapter 1), to whom I continue to be grateful for his inspiration and his willingness to collaborate on a wide range of performance-related projects.

I am deeply grateful for the generosity of each interviewee in this book, and for the enthusiasm of the young actors at Wagner College who kindly spoke about the rehearsal process for their main stage production of *Cats* (Chapter 10).

Without the vision and daring of Australian physiotherapist, Jane Grey, I would not have been able to do the work that opened a critical door to understanding the breath management strategies of vocal performers (Chapter 4).

And without Jane's suggestion I would not have contacted Professor Paul Hodges, in Brisbane, Australia, whose kind invitation and expert guidance led to an exploratory study at the University of Queensland (Chapter 5).

To Dr. Robert Lewis and Dr. Marie-Louise Bird at the University of Tasmania, Launceston, and to students in the Acting program at Tasmanian College of the Arts, sincere thanks for the collaborative spirit that characterized the study in voice and movement in 2013 (Chapter 5).

Heartfelt thanks to Mary Saunders-Barton for writing the Foreword, and to Dr. Kenneth Tom, co-author of *One Voice*, and James Harrison, actor/director and Integrative Studies practitioner, for reading parts of the book and making invaluable comments and suggestions.

Finally, huge thanks to Jennie Morton, performer, osteopath, and specialist in Performing Arts Medicine, for checking many of the chapters for anatomical accuracy and for making suggestions that were immensely helpful.

Joan Melton

Introduction

"Do dancers and singers breathe differently? I've heard they do."

"I can sing it standing, but when I do the movement…"

"This is so much easier. I was doing a lot
of things I didn't need to do!"

(Theatre performance majors, Wagner College, NYC 2015)

In January of 2007, I attended a workshop that changed the course of my life. While it was not a workshop on voice and dance, it opened an analytical door to communication across performance disciplines. *Dancing with Voice* highlights the journey that followed, as it documents collaborations with physiotherapists, dancers, actors, directors, and voice specialists in theatre and music.

A defining moment came early on, in a physiotherapy clinic in London (see Chapter 4), where I was working with Australian physiotherapist, Jane Grey. We were using real-time ultrasound imaging to observe muscle activation patterns of abdominal muscles during voicing in a wide range of physical positions. At our first filmed session, both Jane and I noticed that the deepest muscle, transversus abdominis, and often internal oblique as well, released for inhalation and engaged with the voice. I'd known for a long time that something could release regardless of the physical position, but until then I didn't know what it was.

Then in Pilates and yoga-based positions we saw the multitasking of those same muscles as they moved to effect the positions and continued to work with the voice. So the directive was clear: there had to be a vital connection between voice and dance!

The chapters that follow are individual pieces written since 2007, several of which were published in earlier versions by professional journals or newsletters:

Part I, "Interviews with Dancers," includes conversations with three very different multidimensional performer/teachers: Rusty Curcio, William F. Lett, and Francine Zerfas.

Part II, "Research," looks at groundbreaking research projects in the UK and Australia, respectively, focusing on breath management strategies of performers across a wide range of performance genres.

Part III, "Triple Threats on Dancing with Voice," provides insights into the training and thinking of three young musical theatre performers at different stages of their respective careers.

Part IV, "Research in Motion," details a performance-based project at Wagner College, NYC, and suggests widening the lens in performance training.

Throughout the book, there are references to human anatomy, so having an accurate *body map* will be invaluable to the reader. Books, papers and articles relating to anatomy are included in the Bibliography, along with excellent material on voice, movement and dance techniques.

Reference

Melton, J. "Conversations with Theatre Performance Majors," New York: Wagner College, 2015.

PART I

*I*nterviews
WITH DANCERS

1. Voice and Dance Techniques

An Interview with
Rusty Curcio

Rusty Curcio is a Certified Movement Analyst in the Laban/ Bartenieff System of Movement Studies and heads the dance program at Wagner College, Staten Island, NY. He toured internationally with Les Ballets Trockadero de Monte Carlo for nine years, was then with Les Ballet Grandiva de Russia for two seasons, and performed in New York with Peridance Dance Ensemble and Acanthus Ballet Company. He works regularly in regional theatre and is much in demand as a director/choreographer.

Since 2008, I've had the privilege of working with Rusty on collaborative workshops, research projects, and musical theatre productions. Following are excerpts from a conversation we recorded mid-town Manhattan, on a bright December afternoon.

JM: *The words* alignment, breathing (*or* breath management) range, resonance, articulation, *and* connection *are heard frequently in voice training. Are those same words used in dance, and if they are, what do they mean to a dancer?*

RC: We talk alignment and *placement* together. Alignment is how you're organizing your body parts. In the Laban system, Irmgard Bartenieff uses the principle of *Dynamic Alignment*, which refers to the constant change in body parts as we move and align our body to perform the task. It's an ongoing process and not a static placing of muscles and bones into one position. It's about the fact that the body is always changing its shape and its relationship of muscles and joints—you're writing right now and I'm using my hand—even to do those simple things, there's a change happening through the entire body.

So I would add *placement* to your list. Placement relates to the distribution of weight against gravity and into the ground, whether on your hands or your feet—most of it, of course, is going to be on the feet, but in dance we are using other areas of the body as well as the feet for support. So you put those two things together [alignment and placement], it comes out to dynamic alignment through body organization.

Does the term *dynamic alignment* come from Laban or from Bartenieff?

That is a very specific term from the Bartenieff approach to movement study. She was a student of Laban and heavily worked in the body area. So that was her way of explaining what is going on in the body as movement occurs. Her exercises are not about standing still; they're about movement and mobility.

Placement *in the world of voice suggests something quite different, and may be a term that's on the way out, since we cannot actually* place *the voice anywhere, for example, in the chest or head, or "in the mask."*

Breath management: *Voice teachers often think that dancers don't breathe.*

Breathing is a hard one. Our initial response to difficult movement tasks is to do something we call binding the body, because we want control over the body. So an intellectual response to a difficult moment is to bind and constrict. Now that does affect breath and we're perceived as not breathing. Of course, there is something happening, but we're restricting the full capacity of the breath, mostly out of fear or response to executing a difficult move that requires ultimate control. However, this is where the dancer that doesn't breathe, to me, is still a student, and not a dancer yet. I'm not saying they're not talented, but they're still studying; they haven't figured it all out, because to fully move and be expressive, your body is constantly (the Laban work again) *growing* and *shrinking*. And growing and shrinking are related to your breath. On inhalation you always grow, exhalation you always shrink, so even just in flexion and extension of the body, there is a breath pattern, a breath phrasing that goes along with it. Now the more articulate and in control of those two capacities you become, the more you can make intellectual changes and shifts and choices off of what is the *natural* way of doing it. You can actually go against nature, and then that becomes expressive and it's going to affect the breath and the support and all the other components of movement.

There is an area—for years and years in the dance world, especially the ballet world—they talked about the lateral breath of the back. And I never understood what that was…I understood when they talked about it from the point of view of moving your arms from your back and connecting it to the breath, but that was a muscular sensation. I understood the scapula and how it moved my arm, but I didn't understand the whole breath thing. Now I understand and it goes back to the idea of body organization and how integrated the body's chains of connectivity are.

Breath supports the five chains of connection that are part of Irmgard Bartenieff's Developmental Patterns. They are called *Core Distal Connectivity,* or *Naval Radiation, Head-Tail Connectivity, Upper-Lower Connectivity, Body Half Connectivity,* and *Cross Lateral Connectivity.* It's how you're sending the energy and the breath through the body.

However, there is the anatomical need to compress the lower abdominal muscles when you are doing technically difficult executions such as jumping and turning, because that's what gives you a sense of center, and that's what supports your spine when you're landing your jump. At least from my experience, when I work with singers, they fight compressing the lower abdominal muscles, because they want to be able to release.

On inhalation, yes, but the **lower** *abdominal muscles are the very ones we need to use during voicing. I think it's the upper abs that give us a problem in the singing world—although there are, obviously, widely different approaches to breath management for singing.*

I just get the impression—I'm not saying it's right or wrong—my perception is that the students are saying that their lower abdominal muscles want to be full and released. I see them literally stand and they want to widen as much as possible and bulge here, and what they've told me is, "Well, then I have the most air," and I'm thinking, first of all, your diaphragm's here [under the ribs]…

And the air is in your lungs!

So I never understood that.

Hmm, there are two very common, and contrasting, ways of teaching breath management for singers. Sounds as if you're encountering the **down** **and** **out** *method, where you actually distend the lower abdominals during voicing. The other approach is* **in** **and** **up.**

Pelvic floor.

Yes. I studied with a teacher who taught down and out, and I could certainly make vocal sounds that way, but the approach doesn't seem to go along with dance at all.

I'm sitting here shocked because every other voice person I've worked with, whenever I say in my dance classes (I've now taken it out of my vocabulary), "Press the lower abdominal muscles against the lower spine and resist from the lower spine," they have gone like ballistic.

What isn't good is pulling in at the waist.

Oh, well, that's higher.

Yes, that cuts everything off. But here [lower belly], is exactly where we need the action. I often say, "Lift the pelvic floor." Even that thought, coming from Pilates…

I was given the image, too, that they're a big ball, like a big beach ball, and you know if you squeeze it lower than the middle…

The top gets wider!

And you open up the whole upper body. You are right though. There are the dancers who are still learning what that is and they'll pull in at the waist and constrict in the upper chest.

I think that is what so many singing teachers encounter. I used to see students come into my classes, and they seemed to be pulling everything to the middle: the sternum was low, they were turned out, they were tucked, and I was trying to get them to lengthen and widen and free the voice!

Well, that's the old school ballet training, tucking the pelvis under, when they didn't realize you had the six deep lateral outward rotators, which connect to the ischial tuberosities, the femur and the sacrum. They didn't know about those muscles, so they were using the quadriceps and the gluteus to do the turnout, and you're right, they were doing this [demonstrates tucking the pelvis].

Yes, exactly.

You've actually got to release the pelvis slightly back, then go in and up. And then you're totally free. The minute you tuck under, your legs become bound, which then will cause a binding in the hip socket restricting leg mobility and the ability to shift your weight and move through space.

A lot of it is based off of the fact that the Russians worked on a raked stage. Even in their rehearsal studios—they're all raked, so they're not on a level playing field. They're making postural compensations due to the gravitational pull that is caused by working on a raked stage. But that's not the *right* way. You're supposed to move your legs and breathe. And then, on top of that, what they tell you to do—old school and I was trained this way—is to bring the tip of the ribcage close to these bones (pubic symphysis) but like you're saying, it makes people go down and then you get this tucking of the pelvis. You want to release here in the chest and allow rising and lengthening. But what you want to have the sense of is that these [points] are connected with an elastic band, so they're flexible and they can expand, but they're not totally flapping in the wind. And that's all. It's not a matter of really bringing this to this, but of having tone in this area and the ability to release if needed.

This is really helpful!

What I've come to, working in musical theatre, is that when I address breath with the students, I say to them, "I am not teaching you a breathing *technique*. You're going to go work with a voice teacher who will give you a technique for breathing that is about making a specific tone, possibly, or about things I don't know. I am not at all trying to contradict that. Rather, I'm looking at breath from the foundation of what the body does naturally to move and make sound. And if you can find a way to connect those two things [your vocal technique and what the body does naturally], then your singing will be more expressive.

Do you talk about Range *in dance?*

That's not a very used word. If I had to put a definition to it, it would just be the fact that they're versatile.

Resonance?

No.

Articulation?

Of course, articulation of the body: how clear is your articulation, how specific is the use of your body? If the choreography requires you to move your arm, are you moving just your arm? Fosse is a lot of that. Also the word *specific*, but specific is, I think, a vaguer term; articulation, "Okay, now I understand. I just move from this joint. I don't let my wrist go with that." It's that specific. Where you're turning your head, how are you turning your head? Are you using (ballet word) *epaulement*, shouldering, which is where the shoulders give a slight alignment to the body, or are you just using the head? So that's articulation for us.

Specificity, detail. Connection, *or the acting dimension.*

The word *connection* didn't come up much when I was training. I use it now because I work with actors and it's an acting word, but I don't use it a lot because I find it's too vague. This isn't bad because it stimulates a lot of questions, but I feel there are other ways to get to those questions without just saying, "What do you mean by that?" You hear acting teachers all the time, "Connect to the character." Well, give me some information about the character. What is it I'm doing that's not connecting? That's what I need. So, that's in the research. But as far as just dance, no, we don't use that word a lot.

Are there other major aspects of dance training that you would include in such a list?

Yes! Big words that come up are *Spatial Awareness,* and *Spatial Tension.* So you're dealing with space more. First you deal with *body*, which is the anatomy; then you deal with *shape* (the shapes the body makes and how it relates to itself and other objects in space), which is then connected to the word *articulation.* How am I moving my body and what parts of my body am I moving, and how is it relating to itself: body organization? Then you go into *space* and you start dealing with: where am I going in space, what is my spatial awareness? If I'm reaching there, how much counter tension to keep me on balance is resisting the movement or else I just fall over?

Other words come up: how fast you go, how quiet you go, how quickly you get someplace, how bound you are, how static the position is, or how alive the position is. That's all related to Laban ideas of Body, Effort, Space and Shape.

Then you would certainly go into *dynamics,* which is effort. The more general word is dynamics, or energy; the Laban word is *Effort.* How much energy—*how* am I doing the movement? What's the emotional relationship to it? So we would talk about it from that point of view, but like the emotional expression that is underlying the technical move you're doing. You could talk about connection from the point of view of the actor, if you happen to be playing a role, but very often as a dancer you're not in a role. If you do *Romeo and Juliet,* yes, you can talk to those two dancers about Romeo and Juliet, but very often you're an abstract ballet and you're dealing with efforts, which are the energy and the dynamics, which then send a visceral message to the audience.

Perhaps there is a parallel to absolute music. If I'm playing a concerto, there's not a story line as such, but there are conversations, there are lines of movement *in the music that interact.*

Sure, that's exactly the same thing, and we deal with that especially in choreography class. That's the hardest thing for the young choreographers to do. They love doing the narratives. First we do an abstract movement from the point of view of just creating phrases, and they're fine with that, they're just creating movement based on an image or an idea or a picture. Then we go to a narrative and they're fine because they have a story to tell. But what they have not done: they have not taught the dancer to *perform* the narrative, because there's no effort and no abstract quality to that dance. Dance is not a literal art form; there's no spoken word. You can't say, "Brother, or Mother, Father and Daughter" onstage in dance; you can't. You can put three people up on that stage and you can imply the relationships, but you cannot be that literal with dance, and that's really hard for the students to learn. It's hard for any of us to learn really, but that's the craft.

Anything else on a list?

Yes, one more, there's *phrasing*, which then relates to rhythm and musicality, but phrasing is the word we use and it's big. Now you take everything else that you've learned and you make choices [about] how you're going to put it together, and that's phrasing for us.

How it's put together?

Where you put the slows in the effort, where you change the dynamics. The words *loud* and *soft* are even used in the dance world. Now, obviously we're not loud and soft from a vocal point of view, but our movements can be louder or softer. So where do you make those changes and how long do you hold them? That's all phrasing.

How do these individual aspects of training relate to one another in the learning process, and then in performance?

I think it's so individually based, sometimes even on a daily basis. Where are they at that moment in their brain, what are they scared of, what are they not scared of, what are they comfortable with, and then also, what's going on in their personal life and in their emotions? All of that comes into that moment, and you've got to constantly negotiate that moment by giving them something, one of the areas, and if that area doesn't trigger, then you've got to go somewhere else. And again, one of the really big things that come out of the Laban training is that you're given this incredible number of avenues to get to the same product. And you are constantly negotiating with the system and the participant/student. Even in one class you may be utilizing five [avenues] because you have five different people.

When I asked this question to singing teachers, the response was that in the training process you're more aware of the individual elements, whereas in performance you have to let those go and move beyond. You have to go with whatever you have. You're not thinking technique.

I would certainly agree with that as well. Technique becomes a foundation. But even with performance—maybe I'm thinking from the point of view of a coach/director—even when they're out there and they're doing all of that, you can still give them feedback, and there can still be a dialogue about increasing the expression—not necessarily [making it] better, but increasing the expression.

Do you see common denominators between dance and voice—or apparent contradictions?

I think we've touched on some of the contradictions, even in the dance world itself and in voice, but it's still about expression. And it's about an emotional, intellectual and physical relationship to the craft that you're doing. And if you're only doing one [emotional, intellectual or physical], then something's missing. It's got to be that triumvirate, the three of them together. Otherwise, you don't communicate anything.

Thank you so much, Rusty!

Photograph

Headshot by Todd Carroll

Reference

Melton, J. "Voice and Dance Techniques: How They Relate," An Interview with Rusty Curcio, *VOICEPRINT*, Newsletter of the Australian Voice Association (AVA), 2011, www.joanmelton.com/articles.

2. Putting It All Together!

An Interview with William F. Lett

Perhaps more than any other single course, tap for musical theatre has the potential to integrate dance, voice, and acting skills succinctly and efficiently in performance. Bill Lett is a Master Teacher of musical theatre and a tap specialist in the Department of Theatre and Dance at California State University Fullerton.

For nearly 12 years, Bill and I regularly coached on the same shows at CSUF. Yet, it was only after I began free-lancing again that we sat down to talk about voice and dance and how they connect. Following is a conversation we recorded in 2011, immediately after a Tap I class, which I was privileged to observe.

JM: How is tap different from other genres of dance? Where do you begin?

WL: On the first day of class I focus on physical alignment. I have the students lie on the floor, feet on the ground, knees up about six – seven inches apart, and I talk them through a physical inventory of their body: feeling their body on the floor, heels in alignment with their sit bones, the vertebrae stacked.

When we stand and bring the body to a vertical position, our feet stay apart. This becomes our neutral position—weight evenly distributed on the balls of our feet with our heels off the ground [wearing shoes]. Once standing we try to keep the torso stable, lifted, and full.

Our body is divided into three sections: the head is referred to as the *intellect*, the upper torso [including arms] is the *aesthetic*, and then the pelvis [including the legs] is the *vital*. I encourage students to keep their aesthetic plane open, which assists them to feel their breath and, hopefully, reminds them not to slouch over like a broken candy cane. It's all about finding that sense of center and of lift.

Then we'll experience that physical alignment in motion. For example, that locomotor combination we did today (Flap, Heel, Back Flap, Back Flap, Irish step, Gallop, step): novice tappers with no vital or core connection tend to bend over and their body breaks in half, which for me would obstruct the line of the body and ultimately have an adverse effect on sound, or on the ability to produce sound. Aesthetically, I'm looking for that lengthened position, which ultimately allows for a more even absorption of impact by the knee.

One thing with tap that makes it very different from other dance genres is the *tap break*. Dancers are going to tap their feet off during a designated musical section, demonstrating intricate rhythms and tricks that would be challenging to the most seasoned performers if they were singing while they're tapping. In the classroom combination you saw today, "Doin' the Production Code" from *A Day in Hollywood/A Night in the Ukraine*, they're tapping syllabically, so accenting certain syllables both physically and verbally: "<u>**Nu**</u>dity will <u>**ne**</u>ver be per<u>**mi**</u>tted, as being <u>**ne**</u>cessary **for** the **plot**," which requires a bit more core support while singing.

Aha, and after you told them not to make everything the same, we began to understand what they were saying—they were using operative words. We do it all the time when we speak, but often lose that when we're reading.

Because they're new, they're still learning the musicality of tap—they think it's just a piece of metal on a shoe. But if you hit it with your big toe or your little toe or the tip or the ball, it will make a different sound; it's a musical instrument. So you have to understand that you are accompanying yourself. There are different sounds that can be made with the shoe, as opposed to sounds with the words themselves.

And all of this is part of the composition.

Absolutely it is. That applies to most tap musicals. It's the same with the song "Anything Goes." They're going to flap heel flap heel flap heel flap ball change: All simple steps are used to mark time and introduce the dance vocabulary of the musical number. They're not going to do anything really difficult; they're just going to keep time while they're singing, until they have that dance break. Then they cut loose and it's a different beast.

On the genealogy tree of Tap, there are many branches, but there are two strong, identifiable *roots*. We have Broadway Tap, which I teach here, and we have Rhythm Tap, which is *Jelly's Last Jam, Tap Dogs, The Tap Dance Kid, Stomp*, etc., which has a more urban, rhythmic feel, and is often done *a cappella*, as in the work of the Nicholas Brothers, Savion Glover and Gregory Hines. I often refer to Rhythm Tap, as rapping with metal; it feels more like a jam session. I don't know if you've seen the movie *Tap*. It stars Gregory Hines, Sammy Davis Jr., Jimmy Slyde, Bill

Anagnos, Sandman Sims, Bunny Briggs—a lot of the founding fathers of Tap. There's a scene in the movie where tap becomes a form of communication, a percussive challenge against the piano or against each other. They were really creating rhythms for themselves, versus creating rhythms to support a text; the rhythm *was* their text. In essence, they were sending an action with their feet. It was a contest of one-upmanship. "What is that tap step?" "Well look at this…" "Well, I can add on and make it that." "Where does that go?" Hence a challenge. So unless you're doing a show that calls for that kind of fast, furious, intricate, rhythmic melody of Rhythm Tap, the most common form encountered onstage is Broadway Tap.

In the past I've brought in a couple of rhythm tappers to teach a master class in Tap II, but other than that, I think the students here really need to have those 45 - 50 real, true, basic Broadway tap steps they're going to need for every production of *Anything Goes, Dames at Sea, 42nd Street*, etc.

One of the challenges for a tapper who must sing simultaneously is the absorption of the shock waves that go up the body from the impact on the ground—they have the potential to complicate the [singer's] ability to produce an esthetically pleasing sound. For example, I can flap, "In olden days a glimpse of stocking…" and still produce a sound that is unobstructed by my tapping, by engaging my core in addition to my plié. But as soon as I release my core or increase my impact on the ground, I'm bouncing to the point where my sound is distorting. There are always ways around this. Some Broadway shows enhance the tap sounds with tracks so performers still have the ability to produce a supported sound, accompanied by intricate rhythms and fancy footwork. On the other side of the coin, some shows use microphones on the tap shoe itself to augment the tap sound, which in turn allows the dancer not to have to increase the impact, thus reducing the intrusion on the ability to produce clear vocal sound.

Another option is to have separate singing and tapping choruses. So while it's a challenge, choreographers and musical directors *can* accomplish a great vocal sound while tapping. And that's really the hardest part, because your body serves simultaneously as a percussion (tap) *and* string/wind (vocals) instrument.

Tap/singing is like a tremor really. It's like you're holding a note while your body is bouncing. The secret is in that plié. You have to plié, you have to absorb that impact, you have to engage your core and stay lifted. The harder you tap, the more obstructive you're going to be to the body as an instrument. That's why I always say if you don't plié, you're going to get shin splints—a term used loosely to describe an *overuse injury* characterized by a dull aching pain brought on by exercise. The pain is felt on either the inside or outside of the shinbone (tibia). Repetitive loading of the front lower leg commonly causes shin splints. This is often a result of overtraining.

Do you say anything about breath?

I try to remind them to breathe. Young dancers tend to hold themselves together and they (sucks breath in noisily to demonstrate) and they hold their breath. They have not discovered the concept that breath can *help* you in dance. Use the breath in pirouettes, leaps, lifts, jumps. It forms a conjunction within the body…breath gives you energy.

It's the same thing in tap. You have to find that sense of breath or it becomes stale, rigid; it doesn't have any sense of flow or cyclical nature to it. Without breath the body is not really *living* per se; it's just *there*, and it's held tight. It becomes what I often see in competition dance. I had a young dancer who was a professional and she could have assessed right into Tap II. However, as a result of a conversation I had with her, she decided to take Tap I. She made it through four weeks of class and then wanted out. The reason [for wanting out] was different from the reality, which was that she had no breath in her movement. She was technically very gifted, but so stoic and so strong and so stern, and there was no sense of breath, and it was, "This – is – the – trick – that - I - do – real - ly - well." I have one of those in the class you saw: a brilliant, gifted tapper, but there's no breath there. And as a result, she looks angry, and I told her, "You need to engage a sense of breath, and there's going to be a re-nutrient, so to speak, of oxygen in your brain, and you're going to have to find that place to take a breath and it's going to look like you enjoy what you are doing." When they're not breathing, it looks like they're not enjoying it.

This makes so much sense.

It crosses all genres. Find that breath, use the body's momentum to inhale and exhale every time you move, and when you fight it, you're fighting the movement.

This is what I'm hearing, even from people who teach ballet.

Breath and release, absolutely.... I have observed some pedagogy classes where the use of breath becomes a good tool but it also becomes a crutch, being used as a cue. In a dance we may arrive at a section where there is no music and we're dancing in the silence and it's [demonstrates noisy inhalation], so now we're using that inhalation as a cue. We can still accomplish the same breath at that same exact moment, but it's the quality in which it's approached that makes the difference.

Yes, the noisy inhalation is inefficient, as well as ungraceful. What about range, resonance, articulation, the acting dimension? Do those figure into dance training, or are there different components, for example, spatial awareness?

Spatial awareness is so very important in all forms of dance and all visual art. In my class we have a lack of that right now. You saw when they went across the floor, they have no spatial awareness, they're going to dance right on top of you and they don't care. I think part of that is their being in and out of that moment, and whether they're making it as a collective/ group or just as an individual. They need to take in more of the room instead of their own little bubble.

Resonance, I would say it's going to be easier to get a skull or chest [vocal] resonance out of a tap dancer because the lower the sound, the more reverberation from the tap itself because it happens from bottom up. So [sings] "I Can't Be Bothered Now," from *Crazy for You*, is all up in the chest while he is dancing, because it's lifted here [upper torso] and he's tapping down here, and this [lower torso] stays stable.

You say stable, *but it's still working.*

Oh, it's still moving.

That's all you need.

It's a *degree* of release or a degree of holding onto the abdominals. If you completely release, from my perspective, you're going to look like you're nine months pregnant.

Right.

So you still stay upright in the torso, and you drop the pelvic floor without completely releasing the abdominals. I think of releasing the pelvic floor as down though your *hoo hoo*, through your business, just letting-go down below versus letting go forward, because if you let go forward you lose your core, and if you lose your core you have no sense of support, whether breath or physical. But I think you do have to hold your core and drop your pelvic floor.

I'd be fascinated with ultrasound to see what happens with different modalities of movement and sound. Specifically tap, because I'm of the belief that even though the torso is still stationary, there should be less movement in your vital area than there would be in a modern dancer or a ballet dancer. Because in a balancé we're here [demonstrates] or *port de bras*, and dropping and breathing and releasing, so we're engaging in the spine…

But that's not what you're doing…

Right, it's not liquid. In tap we're still connected, we're still engaged, but there's enough room to take that breath. We're not collapsing in the spine; we're staying lifted.

Over the past few years there has been a surfacing of a vocal technique that I absolutely find undesirable, and I know you do as well, which is that audible inhale in singers. It drives me absolutely crazy, and I want them to understand that for me, if you're going to go [demonstrates gasp], it better be exciting or painful, because that's what you're telling me. But it happens a lot now, and I guess it's part of the new culture of pop sounds. Well, I don't necessarily enjoy it.

Neither do I!

And it bothers me because I think they're defeating the purpose of using breath to drive emotions forward; they're just throwing it out there like an obstacle that has nothing to do with the given circumstances.

Exactly. They're interrupting.

Well, you're gasping, and if you're not dying or it's not a discovery, don't gasp.

What about range?

Range, yes, if I was to choreograph and create a production number, I would say, "Please arrange it so it's bright and lifted in sound. Don't put the vocal line in the bottom range," because if it's going to be a dark, full, heavy sound, most likely it won't be choreographed; the lead melody line has got to be in the top half of the vocal range. Otherwise, it's going to be obstructed by dance.

Articulation. Someone mentioned hands, how everything else can be great but if you've got funky hands there's something wrong with your articulation.

I'm going to say funky hands, or external gestures that are not choreographed, are tension, because they don't know where to place tension. So in tap, I see a lot of beautiful lines, but then I see a lot of hand flicking. Or you watch the dancers lose their core engagement and then they start to bend, or their arms lose length and start to collapse and they start to look like Thanksgiving turkeys on a table.

In tap dancing you have to be loose in the ankle. If you're not loose, if there's tension, you're going to have articulation issues. And if you're thinking about it you're going to be tense. So you have to just physically know what you're doing, where you are going, and you have to remember to breathe.

A lot of students have problems with their left foot, like a piano player will have problems with the left hand, that non-dominant hand, non-dominant foot issue.

I used to practice twice as much with my left hand! What about the acting...

One of the things that I'm passionate about now is the fact that I think dancers have to be the best actors, because when Laurie and Curly can't *say* that they're in love they *sing*, "People will say we're in love;" and when they can't *sing* it, they do the dream ballet—and in that dream ballet you still have to act. You can't just go through the movement and the gestures with this veneered, botoxed face. It defeats the purpose of moving the story and action forward. And we're hearing an excuse quite a bit that is applied to musical theatre actors…"Oh, you're musical theatre." So, maybe your choice is too big, or maybe it's not connected or not grounded to a true moment, maybe it's a little bit more theatricalized than it needs to be, or maybe it's just too theme park, too cheesy. But you know what? That exaggerated, expressive life is a style of theatre itself. I guarantee you it's really hard to be pageant perfect for 45 minutes of a review show, and to keep that smile throughout, your vocal and physical technique in place, and stay connected moment to moment. We need to stop the segregation of dramatic actors and musical theatre actors; we have too many things in common under the umbrella of *actor* to start separating the herd.

On another thread, I think it's time we acknowledged that performers use their bodies in different ways to get what they want, and that there's more than one valid approach to technique.

When was the last time you saw a Hambone routine on a Broadway stage [demonstrates]? We haven't seen that for a long, long time… maybe since *The Will Rodgers Follies* (1991). But all of a sudden *The Scottsboro Boys* arrives on Broadway, the actors are sitting on the edge of a rail car and they are starting to Hambone, and the audience response was overwhelming. This harks back to the Minstrel Show and Vaudeville. It's nothing new, but it's using your body in a different way to create percussive sounds and intricate rhythms.

I think every university dance program should have a voice component, not so much for the world of ballet, but I think in modern it's absolutely imperative. It doesn't have to be spoken word—it can just be sound. Dancers don't understand how to use their voice and how to connect to sound. Adding a vocal component challenges and intimidates most concert dancers, [yet] most are going to work for companies that go into schools and theatres: they bring in kids and they teach them a combination or they do a demonstration; they lecture about the style of dance or the company namesake. They have to *project*, they have to engage the audience, and young children have a very short attention span…so connected sound should be very important to a dancer.

When I was in grad school we had a pedagogy class, and it was my only opportunity to teach anything related to musical theatre, so I taught "Once a Year Day," from *Pajama Game*, and made them sing it, and I made them do a polka. In a matter of 10 minutes they were dying. They didn't know how I was able to have the stamina to sing and dance. How do you do this? When your body is your instrument, anything is possible with practice.

Yes!

Absolutely, when your body's the instrument, it can't be compartmentalized. My voice is my voice, but if I do this [movement], it's going to change the sound that I produce. Everything affects something.

Thank you so much, Bill!

Photograph

Headshot by Megan Bahya-Swanson

Reference

Melton, J, Lett, WF, "Putting It All Together." New York: Voice Theatre Solutions, 2011, www.joanmelton.com/articles.

3. Dancer to Actor to Voice Specialist

An Interview with
Francine Zerfas

Few voice teachers in theatre
or music begin their careers as
professional dancers. Yet that is
indeed what Francine Zerfas
did, and her transitions from
dancer to actor to voice specialist are fascinating.

Francine Zerfas has coached Broadway and Off Broadway productions
and was co-founder of The Tiny Mythic Theatre in New York City. She holds
degrees in drama and creative writing, danced with the Hoovar Uprights,
Rezone Dancers, and The New Dance Ensemble, and currently teaches Voice
and Speech at Sarah Lawrence College, Atlantic Theater Acting Conservatory,
and at Brooklyn College.

It was March 2013, mid-day at Playwrights Horizons Theater School at
New York University's Tisch School of the Arts. Francine had organized a classroom for the interview and we had just an hour before students came pouring
in for the next class, as we continued our conversation in the hallway.

JM: When did you start training as a dancer, and when did you feel you wanted to change directions?

FZ: Good question. I began dancing—I'm not exactly sure how old I was, I think 14 or 15. Unfortunately for me, I started late because I was in the Dakotas. I had wanted to dance since I was five, but that simply wasn't going to happen because I was in an 8,000-person town. There was no culture, nothing like that. Then it happened that a Russian ballerina who called herself "Madame something or other," from Sioux Falls, South Dakota, chose to come to Madison (my home town) and offer a ballet class. My mother, sensing my teenage angst and lost-ness, one day said, "I read that there's a ballet teacher who came to town and I signed you up!" It really was miraculous. My life changed utterly overnight. Everything about me started to make sense when I took ballet class. I was too old to be a ballerina, but I didn't care.

After high school, I left the Dakotas and moved to Minneapolis to train. I thought I was just going to take ballet class, but then I was introduced to modern dance, which opened my eyes again. I studied Graham. That was probably the modern dance technique that was most suited to my body because I have a long torso. Loved it, loved it, loved it! I took three different classes a day and in a couple years apprenticed for a time. There aren't a lot of dance companies in Minneapolis, but there are many choreographers there. So, I began dancing and performing in independent works.

At that time, I was also a member of a dance company called the Hoovar Uprights. We even had our own rock 'n' roll band, The Psychenauts. It was actually very theatrical with a great sense of humor. The choreographer, Denise Gustafson, was a brilliant, athletic dancer. She was very original in her work, choreographed dances based on the movement of The Flintstones TV show, and dances where we had to read our moves from cue cards—reminds me a bit of Judson Church dance [New York City].

I think what happened was, at one point in Minneapolis, I had roommates who were visual art students. They were painters, photographers, video makers—they, too, were multitaskers. I started to meet a lot of visual artists and found myself in their films, photos, and performance art pieces. So the idea of performance was beginning to change and now included visuals and language. Eventually, I found myself in Berlin, Germany, with my boyfriend for what turned out to be many months, and that changed me. He was a painter, writer and filmmaker, studying German at the Goethe Institute. I was just the girlfriend who followed him and had a chance to go to Europe for the first time in my life.

The world opened up again, even wider. I tried to take ballet class, but was too scared as I didn't know German, plus I had very little money. So I stopped dancing during that time and did things I'd never done before, like stay in bed for three days reading a book. My friend and I—at that time the Berlin Wall was up—made an art installation, so to speak, on the Berlin Wall. And I started writing, I think because it was very difficult there, but very profound. I was learning about my young self.

I came back to Minneapolis, was accepted into a company as an understudy, the New Dance Ensemble. So I returned to dance. Not long after that, I was observing a rehearsal of a musical that a friend was choreographing, an avant-garde musical. During that rehearsal their lead actor quit and I suddenly found myself singing in a musical and playing a transgendered guy. I don't know how I ever got the nerve to say, "Yes"! I had no idea what I was doing. It was spectacular fun and it turned out I could sing—ish. When I returned to dance rehearsals, I found myself feeling that dance no longer expressed enough for me—that seems like an awfully lofty thought, but it is true. Words became important to me, and visuals. So I decided I was going to try and come to New York to go to acting school.

Where did you go to school?

Undergraduate school, I went to NYU, and actually my graduate degree is in creative writing. My first full-length play was directed by my dear friend of many years, Kristin Marting. We, along with two of our peers, Tim Maner and Kristin Ames, formed a theatre company called The Tiny Mythic Theatre, which really had its birth during our time at Harvard, when we were guest artists and teaching assistants. Years later, after I had left the company to be a freelance actor, that company merged with HOME for Contemporary Arts and is now the theatre, HERE Arts Center, in New York City. At NYU, one of my best teachers and my most important acting teacher was my voice teacher. I have to say I learned the most from that man.

Was that Chuck Jones?

Chuck Jones. Yes. He liked dancers in his classroom, which makes sense. He was a man who not only had a partner who was a dancer, but if you went to his house, you'd find he had a Pilates machine in his bedroom! He was serious about using his body as an actor. I think what he liked about dancers is that dancers are disciplined, they work hard, they know how to practice and listen. You ask them to do something and they'll do it. Voice work was yet another physical skill that showed me what more was possible. It is cheesy to say he gave me my voice, but it is true. He gave the nasally, tight-jawed girl from the Prairie a voice. He invited me to train with him as a teacher, and so I did for a number of years. Then he sent me off on my own path with the words "Make it your own." Ask how I made that transition? That's how I can make sense of that journey.

And of course, you use everything in your life in your teaching

That is absolutely the case.

...and in your performing.

Yes. When I finally figured out how to move as an actor, I found that movement only improved my experience of acting and was the tool that helped me understand my voice beyond my training.

That is gold, especially for people who think movement is something against voice.

I did appreciate, when reading Catherine's [Fitzmaurice] essay, "Breathing is Meaning," the phrase, "Voice is an action." That was a really profound statement that helped me understand the idea that it's my *body* in action. And that, I think, is also my strength as a teacher. In my Fitzmaurice work I've been called *athletic* in my teaching. I think of voice work as a very athletic experience. I know the body from my own experience of it—from a girl with seven brothers who could play any sport they could, a dabbler in gymnastics in grade school, to a dancer, an actor, and a long-time student of yoga and Pilates. My approach to voice is from this strong movement understanding, and a very technical understanding. I by no means understand the anatomy like you do.

You understand at a deep level.

I understand at a very intuitive level and I do my best to educate myself. And I trust my instincts—well, most of the time. What keeps me intrigued in teaching voice is that, as you say, everything I do, and have done, comes into my classroom. I've just finished reading Patti Smith's recent book about her and Mapplethorpe when they were kids in New York City. I started listening to her music again, which I hadn't heard in over twenty years. I was astounded at what I was hearing now, not only at this age, but also with this ear and knowledge. I watched her performances in the '70s on YouTube and was in awe at what she was doing with language, with her body, and her voice. I'm bringing that into my classroom, asking my students to lie back and just listen to her sing "Birdland." Talk about body in action, from tongue to toe.

I think I do teach what I'm interested in, and I teach what I want to learn, as well as what I know. I am finding my own way in my teaching, and movement and language are primary. I've learned a lot along the way.

I understand dancers. It's possible to dance, sing and act. You don't have to throw the rest away just because you want to act as well.

I can remember at NYU, when I was an acting student, trying to do a class exercise—I'm not exactly sure what the exercise was, something like take an object and tell a story about it while moving. (It was still early in the stage of transitioning from dance to acting.) I have always thought of a dancer as an architect of space and an actor as inhabiting the body differently. I'm not sure if I even know how to express this. It's not about design and it's not about an extension of limbs in space. In this object exercise, I felt I could do anything with my body and this object, but my teacher kept saying "But there's no story. You're not connected to it." What does that *mean*? What is it I'm not doing? What does *connection* mean?

When I saw *Pina*, the movie, I was so moved. I laughed, I cried, I longed. I have to say that when I saw that, I really felt that if I had known about her when I was dancing, that would have been the company—and if I had better legs and feet—that would have been the company for me. I feel her work is both dance and theatre. In the movie, Pina was interviewed about her role in *Café Muller*. She spoke about her experience when rectifying that role and how in rehearsal she knew that something was missing but couldn't figure out why it didn't feel right. (What's important to know about that role is that she was dancing with her eyes closed in a café filled with chairs and tables that the dancers were constantly moving around.) She explained that she discovered that there was a difference when her eyes were closed if she was looking down or looking up. So, where the eyeballs were positioned completely informed her interior life, and that was what she was missing. Ah, how amazing. That is the transition from dance to acting. It is about moving internally. And yet, she did both.

How long have you been teaching?

I think I started in 1991. I was first trained in Chuck Jones' work and co-taught classes with him for a time before being allowed my own classes. He was a generous guy. I taught that work for many years before training in Fitzmaurice work. When I was finishing my certification with Catherine, she asked me what and where I was teaching. I was teaching Chuck's work, which is based in Iris Warren and Kristin Linklater's work, and I was trying to figure out how to bring Fitzmaurice into my teaching, which I've been doing now for about eight years. I have a much better understanding of what I'm doing now and why I think it's important. My students really dig it. They see, like I, the merit of both and how they are complimentary. I remember, when answering Catherine's question, she responded by saying she thought her work was very complimentary with other techniques. I was really grateful for that. I am fully committed to Chuck's work and don't consider my voice worked out sufficiently without it. I think his "channel" work continues to change my voice. But Catherine's work appeals to the dancer in me, and has connected me to the deep interior of my voice through my body.

As a vocal coach, when you have an actor who sings and dances, or an actor who's not a dancer but can move well and has to act, I began to think, "Wait a minute, I still don't have the right equation." Then I realized we simply have to be adaptable. I've done a good amount of movement/theatre, whether it was a devised piece or a new interpretation of a play, and have come against that issue of speaking and moving a great deal without much awareness. But as a teacher, I've had to wrestle with this in order to open up my students' voices and get them to meet the demands of the play or production.

You've had a fascinating career, with some remarkable changes of perspective. Any thoughts about where you go from here?

I think what inspires me now is *language*, both written and spoken. I love rich, poetic language of any kind, and greatly enjoy working with my students from all over the world who come to Atlantic Theater to study. I love hearing the difference in their sounds and voices. And I feel that working with them has opened my ear to another level of beauty in the voice.

How exciting! It will be interesting to see where that inspiration leads.

Thank you so much, Francine!

Photograph

Headshot by Tiny Mythic Theatre Company, Tim Maner, Director

Reference

Melton, J. "Dancer to Actor to Voice Specialist: An Interview with Francine Zerfas." Routledge: *Voice & Speech Review*, 2014; *VOICEPRINT*, Newsletter of the Australian Voice Association, 2013.

PART II

Research

4. Ab Prints and the Triple Threat

In January 2007, voice professionals from around the world gathered at the Royal Academy of Dramatic Art (RADA), London, for a Conference on Performance Breath. Over several days, participants were given splendid opportunities to interact, both at plenary sessions and at a wide variety of workshops. I was particularly intrigued by a workshop entitled, "Ultrasound Imaging of the Abdominal Support Mechanisms whilst Voicing," led by physiotherapists Ed Blake and Jane Grey, of PhysioEd Medical, London:

> [The presenters] demonstrated...the advantages of Real Time Ultrasound in assessing abdominal muscular patterns while voicing, and consequently the effect of poor support...This Real Time approach is ground breaking in its speed to diagnose and see the problems (Hawkins 2007, 8).

Working with volunteers, Blake and Grey focused on the *transversus abdominis* (the deepest layer of superficial abdominal muscle) to be sure it was active during normal conversation. They explained that if the *obliques* were working without the transversus, there would likely be compensatory muscle contractions elsewhere in the respiratory-phonatory system to effect the needed respiratory drive to produce the desired voicing:

> The overriding clinical presentation is of over activity of the sternocleidomastoid musculature and secondary tightness of the suprahyoid soft tissue resulting in an elevated larynx in resting position and poor cricothyroid mobility (Hawkins 2007, 8).

This seemed to verify Zemlin's suggestion (1988) that, because of their location and fiber direction, transversus would have more to do with exhalation, and obliques with postural stability of the torso in space. However, as I work primarily with healthy voices in actor training, I wanted to know how abdominal muscles responded and performed in physically demanding circumstances. So after the conference I met with Jane Grey, put myself under investigation (Figure 4.1), and saw—perhaps for the first time ever—the abdominal muscle activity for laughing, crying, shouting and other extended voice use, as well as for speaking and singing in a variety of physical positions. The equipment for observing abdominal activity during extended physical movement has not yet been developed.

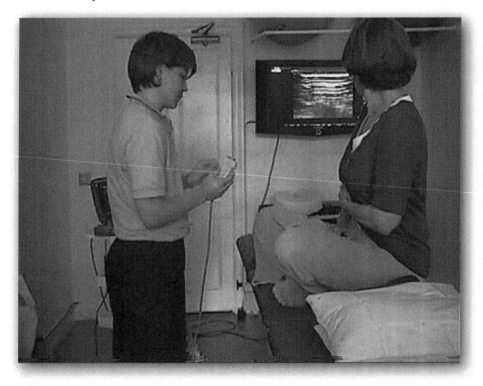

Following that initial session, Jane and I conducted pilot studies to determine the specifics of abdominal muscle activity for nine other subjects. Seven of those were trained performers (including three major teachers of singing for musical theatre); two were fit adults with no prior voice training. In addition, we looked at the abdominal activity of an advanced trumpet player, while playing, and found it to be highly similar to that observed in the breath management of singers.

Continued research involving a larger cross section of populations will be required before these preliminary findings can be generalized. However, at least two very interesting observations may be mentioned at this point:

First: The transversus abdominis (Figure 4.2) can release and engage, even when remaining superficial abdominal muscles (internal and external obliques and rectus abdominis) are involved in maintaining postural stability in the mid-lower torso, e.g., in a Pilates V (Figure 4.3).

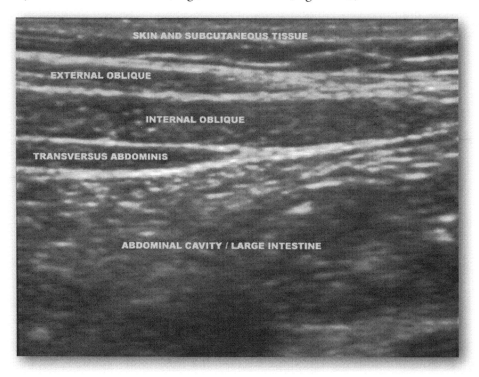

SKIN AND SUBCUTANEOUS TISSUE

EXTERNAL OBLIQUE

INTERNAL OBLIQUE

TRANSVERSUS ABDOMINIS

ABDOMINAL CAVITY / LARGE INTESTINE

This information is enormously useful for voice/movement specialists, and may have particular relevance to musical theatre performance.

It is important to note that engagement of the transversus appears to be spontaneous in normally functioning subjects, although less conscious and decisive in individuals not trained as performers. Also, activation of the transversus may be queued from different points in the torso (e.g., from the pelvic floor, or from the lower abdomen), and the fact of its engagement tells us very little about the overall technique of the performer.

The critical part of the equation for all the abdominals seems to be a *release* of muscle contraction after exhalation, to facilitate a more efficient inhalation. That release, far more than engagement, frequently needs attention in the technical training of actors and singers, and in the vocal training of dancers.

Second: Each subject seems to have a unique "ab print," or basic neuromuscular pattern that may be seen to a greater or lesser degree, regardless of the vocal/physical task. Overall, observation suggests that transversus tends to take the lead in any activity, with internal and external obliques, in that order, coming in to assist whenever necessary. In certain extended voice use, e.g., laughing and crying, the rectus abdominis is also involved.

While this represents only a preliminary set of observations based on a small sample size, it opens the door to an almost unlimited variety of full-scale projects and collaborative designs. In addition, it calls attention to the physicality of voice work and to the extraordinary range of vocal sounds that are essential to the actor's repertoire.

Practical Applications

Although we have examined only one part of the total instrument, focusing on the physical core is both critical and timely, especially in the training of musical theatre performers. When the abdominal/pelvic "center" is overlooked, activity in the upper body (shoulders, chest, neck and head) frequently attempts to compensate for a lack of awareness and use of the lower torso.

In *Communicating Voice,* March 2008, Janice Chapman says:

> Again and again I have found that intervening at the level of the torso to correct breathing and support problems has resulted in the vocal fold and resonance problems either disappearing altogether, or being able to be resolved quickly and easily. For example...[jaw and tongue root tension] problems resolve very quickly (and stay resolved) once a singer has been introduced to some Accent Method work to free up their air followed by work on postural alignment and abdominal support.

The Accent Method was developed by Svend Smith in Denmark for use in voice therapy, and is a brilliant addition to the technical tools of a voice teacher or coach. Repeated rhythmic patterns (with accents) are employed, first with unvoiced fricatives, then with other sounds—rather like staccatos in rhythm—to wake up and train the abs.

One of the most valuable skills gained in an Accent Method approach is the ability to let go quickly, or to release the abdominal muscles—albeit only partially in some strenuous positions—so that the need for an upper chest "top up," or "catch breath," is eliminated.

In *Singing and the Actor*, Gillyanne Kayes says:

> A very wise singing teacher told me during my training that the secret of breathing in was to breathe out... [Exercises based on the Accent Method] engage the muscles of active expiration, and they will help you to release the abdominal wall so that you can breathe in fast and efficiently.

In addition to relieving stress in the upper body and solving technical problems, use of the abs is key to our experiencing a character as a whole person, rather than as a "talking head." Mel Churcher, who coaches and directs the gamut of theatre venues, frequently asks an actor who is working on a TV monologue to place a hand on the abdomen the second time through the piece. That simple action changes the sound and impacts communication immediately, so that both actor and coach are working at a different level very quickly.

In the second stage of the ultrasound project—which moves now to Australia—we are focusing on vocal performers in different media (e.g., opera, jazz, folk, as well as musical theatre) and on the technical connections between voice and dance. Although "performance breath" for singing has traditionally been considered incompatible with certain aspects of dance technique(s), the triple threat must marry the two. And as we begin to examine dance and voice work *together*, the common denominators appear! What those are and how they interact in performance will be the subject of future articles.

My interest in the use of ultrasound imaging while voicing springs from a desire to know the "truth" about what we do and what we teach. Voice training is and has been fraught with myths, and some of those myths have been useful at times. Yet, when we are able to sort out what actually happens in even one aspect of the technical process, we are then freed to make subtle adjustments in our understanding of the whole mechanism.

Photographs

Photography by Gerard Reidy

References

Blake, E, Grey, J. "Ultrasound Imaging of the Abdominal Support Mechanisms whilst Voicing," Performance Breath, RADA/BVA, January 2007.

Chapman, J. "Speaking Out – Janice Chapman replies..." *Communicating Voice,* Vol. 8 (3), March 2009, 9.

Churcher, M. "Breath for Screen Acting," Performance Breath, RADA/BVA, January 2007.

Harris, D, Harris, S. "The Accent Method: An Introduction to Abdominal Breathing and Support," Performance Breath, RADA/BVA, January 2007.

Hawkins, C. "The Mechanics of Breathing as Applied to Different Vocal Tasks," *Communicating Voice,* Vol. 8 (1), August 2007, 8.

Kayes, G. *Singing and the Actor,* 2nd ed. London: A & C Black (UK), New York: Routledge (USA and Canada), 2004, 29.

Melton, J. "Ab Prints and the Triple Threat," VOICE*Prints,* NYSTA Newsletter January-February, 2009, 6 – 7.

Smith, S, Thyme, K. *Die Akzentmethod.* Vedback: The Danish Voice Institute, 1981.

Zemlin, W. *Speech and Hearing Science,* 3rd ed. Boston: Allyn & Bacon, 1988, 73 – 75.

5. Breath Management Strategies across Performance Genres

March – May of 2010, a groundbreaking exploratory research study took place at the University of Queensland (UQ), in Brisbane, Australia. Following up on pilot research in London (see Chapter 4), the study at UQ focused on breath management strategies of professional performers across seven vocal genres: acting, classical singing, musical theatre, jazz, pop, rock and country.

A primary goal of the study was to open up research to a larger range of vocal performers. Nearly all voice research until that time had been with classical singers. Although a few studies had focused on country singers in the US (Cleveland et al, 1997, Hoit et al, 1996, Stone et al, 1999, Sundberg et al, 1999), neither actors nor musical theatre performers, nor jazz, pop or rock performers had been given similar attention.

A secondary goal was to compare observations from Brisbane with those made in London and to note similarities and differences across performance genres

Twenty-eight professional vocal performers participated in the study; three researchers from the lab at UQ served as controls. Professor Paul Hodges, of the School of Health and Rehabilitation Sciences, was the Chief Investigator and I coordinated the study.

In addition to real time ultrasound imaging, surface electromyography (EMG) was used to monitor electrical activity associated with muscle contraction for three abdominal muscles: rectus abdominis, external oblique, and internal oblique. Intramuscular EMG with fine wire electrodes was used with 26 subjects in order to record from the transversus abdominis. As this muscle is deep, its activity cannot be recorded with electrodes placed on the skin. Instead, a small wire similar in diameter to human hair was inserted into the muscle with a needle guided by ultrasound imaging. Once the electrode was in place the needle was removed, leaving the hair-like wire in the muscle until the end of the experiment, when it was withdrawn.

Inductive plethysmography was used to measure movements of the chest and abdominal walls: Respitrace (light-weight, elastic) bands were placed around the upper and lower trunk at the levels of the navel and mid chest. The entire project was filmed and a brief, recorded interview with the respective subject was conducted prior to each experiment.

While a relatively still position was used for most common tasks, subjects were asked to perform repertoire in positions and/or movement as close to their usual manner as possible (Figure 5.1).

Observations

Early in the process, we noted a direct relationship between transversus abdominis (TA) and the vocal sound. This was not unexpected, as the project in London had revealed a similar pattern of TA engagement for voicing and release for inhalation. However, as the work progressed we began to see other patterns as well, so further investigation, analysis, and documentation of muscle activation patterns is clearly needed.

Also as in London, rectus abdominis seemed relatively uninvolved in breath management while internal and external obliques appeared to work independently, rather than as a unit, the internal muscle frequently acting as sidekick to transversus and the external muscle serving more of a postural function. However, as these actions were not consistent across genres, further investigation is needed.

The greatest excursion of abdominal muscles—wide release for inhalation and clear contraction for voicing—was seen in actors and classical singers via ultrasound imaging. Considerably less movement was observed for jazz and contemporary singers, while musical theatre, crossover and triple threats fell somewhere in between. Although larger populations would be required to generalize any of these preliminary findings, likely contributing factors to observed differences are:

- Necessity to be heard without amplification for classical styles
- Regular amplification of jazz and other contemporary styles
- Long phrases required in classical material, both sung and spoken
- Use of relatively short phrases in musical theatre and contemporary
- Differences in registration and vocal set-up among styles
- Physical/postural differences from one performance environment to another
- Differences in breath management strategies

A DVD is available showing 19 excerpts from the ultrasound sessions, organized by category.

Again early in the process, inductive plethysmography (Respitrace) showed a pattern of contrast between movements in the chest and abdominal walls. Whereas the ribcage seemed to float down gradually throughout a single exhalation, individual abdominal muscles appeared to be directly involved with phrasing, inflection, and word stress. Therefore, movements of the chest wall were relatively smooth while movements of the abdominal wall were more jagged.

Then as the study progressed, we began to see other patterns, including what appeared to be greater involvement of the chest wall in phrasing. However, as these differing patterns were not clearly related to genre and, in some cases, may have been unique to individual performers, additional investigation with larger populations is needed.

One possible contributing factor to abdominal and chest wall movements, as well as to abdominal activation patterns, was not considered at the time of the study, but surfaced later: Several performers tucked, or tilted the pelvis (posterior rotation) as part of their vocal technique. Consequently, abdominal muscles regularly involved in breath management for voicing were multi-tasking to effect the backward tilt of the pelvis. An article written in 2011 (see Chapter 6) explores this topic.

Related Work

In 1989, a study by Watson, Hoit, Lansing and Hixon, "Abdominal Muscle Activity during Classical Singing," noted minimal use of rectus abdominis and considerable activity in lateral abdominals (external oblique (EO), internal oblique (IO), and transverse, or some combination of these muscles). However, as only surface electrodes were used, Watson et al were able to determine only regional activity:

> …abdominal activation during singing is clearly regional. Specifically, the lateral region of the abdomen is highly active, whereas the middle region is not. Differential activation of the upper and lower portions of the lateral abdomen also is characteristic of singing, *with the most common*

pattern being characterized by greater activation of the lower portion relative to the upper portion [italics added]. These regional differences are essentially the same in kind as those associated with resting tidal breathing and speaking, and therefore, are not singing-specific.

Particularly significant re vocal technique were observations: (1) that the lower portion of the lateral abdomen (IO) was more active than the upper (EO), and (2) that observed regional differences were the same as those associated with tidal breathing.

As studies since 1989, including those in London and Brisbane, have reported internal oblique frequently mirroring transversus, greater activity in the lower portion of the lateral abdomen would be expected. Moreover, during the London project, we observed essentially the same muscle activation patterns (as in tidal breathing) in untrained subjects as in highly trained professionals.

In 2012, a study in the UK, "An Investigation of Abdominal Muscle Recruitment for Sustained Phonation in 25 Healthy Singers," by Macdonald, Rubin, Blake, Hirani and Epstein, focused on baseline muscle thickness and recruitment patterns of transversus and internal oblique during semi-supine (knees up, feet on the floor) phonation in a range of vocal qualities (not to be confused with vocal *genres*, which include the life and work of the performer).

Macdonald et al found that although there were greater changes in millimeter thickness of internal oblique, percentage changes were consistently greater in transversus: TA was "recruited preferentially and significantly in most vocal qualities tested (2012, 1)."

Practical Applications

April of 2013, I returned to Australia, this time to Tasmania to lead a voice/movement project at Tasmanian College of the Arts, University of Tasmania (UTAS), Launceston. An ultrasound component of the project included collaboration with Dr. Marie-Louise Bird, physiotherapist and Lecturer from the School of Health Sciences, and with Dr. Robert Lewis, Lecturer in Theatre, Tasmanian College of the Arts.

Soon after arriving, I discovered that participants in the project (seven actors in training) had considerable experience in a wide range of movement modalities, including Suzuki, Butoh and Laban. However, their knowledge and experience of voice that included singing, was more limited. So in order to observe and document a relationship between their physicality and voicing, substantial work needed to be done in the area of vocal production in a movement-based context.

During a total of 12 class hours, supplemented by individual sessions, we were able to make excellent progress in a relatively short time, and during the last week of the project, participants observed a range of voice/movement tasks using ultrasound imaging (Figure 5.2).

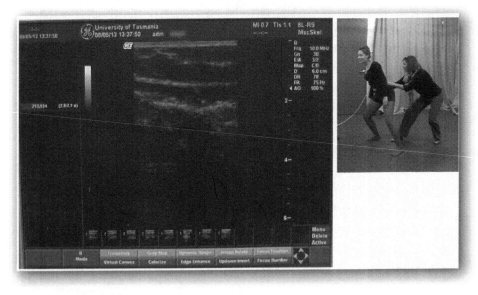

Efficient breath management was key to connecting voice, including singing, to movement as well as to text. And the vocal possibilities of range, resonance, power and intimacy facilitated by that efficiency, changed the relationship of voice to the rest of the participants' work.

The most important lesson for me in the UTAS experience was that *integration* requires knowledge and skill in every area that is being integrated. Put another way and more directly, excellent movement training will not produce great vocal skills; nor will great voice training produce excellent movement skills. However, voice and movement truly integrated can lift the level of performance in every aspect of an actor's work.

Summary

Recent studies into breath management across performance genres have helped to clarify certain aspects of what we do and what we teach as practitioners. Several items appear to have a direct relation to voice, movement and dance in performance:

1. Transversus abdominis, which interdigitates with the diaphragm, tends to work directly with the voice, releasing for inhalation and engaging for voicing.
2. Internal oblique frequently co-contracts, or works with, transversus, so that the physical action noted by the performer may be in the lateral region of the lower abdomen.
3. External oblique tends to have more of a postural function, and rectus abdominis appears to be only minimally involved in breath management.
4. As muscles regularly multi-task, abdominal muscles involved in managing the breath for voicing may be simultaneously involved in moving the body through space.

Photographs

Figure 5.1 by Joan Melton; Figure 5.2 by Christopher Jackson

References

Cleveland, T, Stone, RE, Sundberg, J, Iwarsson, J. "Estimated Subglottal Pressure in Six Male Country Singers," *Journal of Voice*, 11 (4), 1997, 403 – 409.

Hoit, JD, Jenks, CL, Watson, PJ, Cleveland, TF. "Respiratory Function during Speaking and Singing in Professional Country Singers," *Journal of Voice*, 10 (1), 1996, 39 - 49.

Macdonald, I, Rubin, JS, Blake, E, Hirani, S, Epstein, R. "An Investigation of Abdominal Muscle Recruitment for Sustained Phonation in 25 Healthy Singers," *Journal of Voice*, 26 (6), 2012, 815. e9 – e16.

Stone, RE, Cleveland, T, Sundberg, J. "Formant Frequencies in Country Singers' Speech and Song," *Journal of Voice*, 13 (2), 1999, 161 – 167.

Sundberg, J. Cleveland, T, Stone, RE, Iwarsson, J. "Voice Source Characteristics in Six Premiere Country Singers," *Journal of Voice*, 13 (2), 1999, 168 – 183.

Watson, P, Hoit, J, Lansing, R, Hixon, T. "Abdominal Muscle Activity during Classical Singing," *Journal of Voice*, 3 (1), 1989, 24 – 31.

6. Tucking the Pelvis: Actual and Perceived Outcomes

Fall 1989, as I stood waiting for a train in London, I diligently reminded myself to tuck the pelvis under. I'd decided that was the way to counteract a tendency toward overarching, or being sway backed. Then, one day, after table work at an Alexander lesson, I stood up and the tutor said, "How do you feel?" I said, "I feel like I'm sticking my tail out." He said, "No, now you're aligned!"

Later, in university classes, first-year students regularly came in straight from dance class, stood in first position, sternum dropped, and pelvis tucked. And I was trying to get them to lengthen and widen and free the voice!

So my Pilates teacher, who also taught ballet and chaired a dance program, suggested I have the students stand parallel and relevé, leading with the pelvis and making sure not to rock back on their heels when they came down. Almost instantly, the tuck was gone, sternum was lifted—and she assured me dancers needed to be able to work parallel as well as turned out.

In an interview in 2008, dancer/choreographer and movement analyst, Rusty Curcio, explained the physicality I'd observed in my students:

> That's the old school ballet training, tucking the pelvis under, when they didn't realize you had the six deep lateral outward rotators, which connect to the ischial tuberosities, the femur and the sacrum. So they were using the quadriceps and the gluteus to do the turnout…A lot of it is

based off the fact that the Russians worked on a raked stage, so not on a level playing field…On top of that, they told you to bring the tip of the ribcage as close to these bones [pubic symphysis] as possible, but it makes people go down and so you get this tucking of the pelvis…You've actually got to release the pelvis slightly back, and then go in and up. Then you're totally free. The minute you tuck under, your legs become bound, which then will cause a binding in the hip socket restricting leg mobility and the ability to shift your weight and move through space.

Under "Posture Myths that Cause Mismapping" (*What Every Singer Needs to Know about the Body*, Plural 2009, 46), MaryJean Allen writes:

[Tucking] the pelvis under…ruins the rebound of the abdominal wall and pelvic floor and prevents spinal lengthening. It also tightens the hip joints as well as the buttock and leg muscles, compromising the movements of breathing and singing and all leg movements.

And in her classic text, *Inside Ballet Technique: Separating Anatomical Fact from Fiction in the Ballet Class* (1994, 39 - 40) Valerie Grieg says:

[The] position of the pelvis…affects the functioning of the entire body… Anatomists…describe the movements of the pelvis from the top of its front rim, so that when you drop your hip bones and stick out your tail, the pelvis is said to be tilting forward. Conversely, when you flatten your back and tuck your tail, the pelvis is said to be tilted back. Both of these aberrant positions are highly undesirable.

The forwardly tilted pelvis, usually accompanied by flaccid abdominal muscles, results in a hollow back…it causes a compensatory increase in the thoracic curve, which results in a protruding rib cage and impaired breathing…Even more destructive is the tucked or backwardly tilted pelvis, which occurs almost invariably in response to the instruction "grip your buttocks." The lamentable effects are all pervading. The reversal of the curve in the lumbar spine causes the other curves to flatten excessively, reducing the spine's flexibility and capacity for absorbing shock.

Yet, many excellent singers, and even actors, tuck the pelvis as a regular part of their vocal technique. In a recent study (Brisbane 2010) involving professional performers from a range of vocal genres, participants were asked whether or not they tucked the pelvis and what they perceived as benefits from either tucking or not tucking. Several respondents indicated a perceived postural effect, as well as a connection to breath management and voice quality:

[Classical singer] I guess the reason for tucking is to get the whole body involved. As there are a lot of muscles in the pelvic floor, [tucking] acts as a support system to technique…line, legato, breath control, etc., and makes it easier to sing because the focus is off the throat and the technique sits more into the body.

[Actor] I was never told to tuck in dance or voice but to create a *neutral* spine. I think I may have done this by tucking a little bit due to the curve of the back. It does help alignment and my lower abs engage.

[Musical theatre performer] Personally I don't use pelvic tuck. I think I engage the lower abdominal muscles a lot, but not quite pelvic floor. I do find that if I squeeze my butt muscles together I can have more strength in my sound…but I don't use it very often. I just use a more general abdominal muscle support.

[Crossover singer] When I first started movement training, it was my impression that I was out of alignment and that tucking the pelvis under was bringing it into alignment. I eventually went too far and since have come back. I think the tilt or tuck is a vocal thing…and there are other ways of getting pelvic floor to happen.

Mention of the word *tilt* seemed to suggest the possibility of a different action. In *Singing and Teaching Singing* (Plural 2006, 27 – 28), Janice

Chapman speaks of "slightly tilting" the pelvis without clenching the buttocks, which, in her words, "helps to engage the lower abdominal and pelvic floor muscles in a posturally advantageous setting." However, Chapman also advocates use of the SPLAT (Singers Please Loosen Abdominal Tension) in-breath, which requires a "flexible abdominal wall." Tight hip joints, buttock and leg muscles accompanying a pelvic tuck would seem to preclude that flexibility.

Perhaps the critical difference between *tuck* and *tilt* is gripping the buttocks. In *Your Voice: An Inside View* (Inside View 2004, 103), Scott McCoy says, "Many singers and teachers attribute an expiratory function to…the *gluteus maximus*, [although these muscles] have no actual ability to compress the contents of the abdomen [and] should not be considered legitimate expiratory muscles."

Some respondents clearly differentiated between *tucking* and *tilting*:

[Crossover singer] *Tilting* is a very specific and isolated movement that does not involve the buttocks. I often think of it as the "oo" moment in line dancing.

[Pop singer] I definitely *tuck* when I anchor for a big note. I find this tightening of the buttocks enables me to have a stronger supported core.

[Country-pop singer] *Tucking* gives my voice more strength all round. I find it easier to control my volume and my voice tends to be much smoother too.

[Actor/director] If done subtly, *tilting* can improve posture… Obviously, this can lead to holding, especially around the belly wall, and even up into the ribcage, so it's essential to appreciate the difference between folding everything up, as it were, and simply engaging the internal core muscles, isolating those as far as possible from the outer, more easily recognized muscle groups.

So, there are apparently two different, but related pelvic actions that may, in some cases, work on a continuum from subtle to gripping. And the performers quoted mention (overall) three specific aspects of vocal technique—alignment, breathing, and resonance—as being directly affected by the action(s) they choose to employ.

Still others performers reported neither tilting nor tucking:

> [Crossover singer/teacher] Re tucking, I'm not one, but when younger dabbled until I realized what I really needed was better alignment. As a teacher, I find many young people with alignment issues that are very problematic (endemic probably of our computer/desk-centric lives). I tend to think of the tuck as a quick fix that doesn't help in the long term.
>
> I also gave tilting a good go, being someone who had a sway back, but never really felt comfortable. There were many other things that needed to be done to align my body, and once they were dealt with…success!

In *Respiratory Function in Singing: A Primer for Singers and Singing Teachers* (2006, 105 – 106), Thomas Hixon writes:

> A common working assumption in singing pedagogy is that straighter alignment of the vertebral column and torso will ensure better respiratory function…The vertebral column has natural curvatures in it and the muscles of the respiratory apparatus have certain preferred mechanical advantages in relation to those natural curvatures…Not only does unnatural straightening…affect the range of volumes, pressures and shapes that can be attained, it can also negatively influence the flexibility of performance.

Since both anatomists and movement specialists assert that tilting the pelvis either forward or backward works *against* efficient alignment and that tucking the pelvis (defined to include tightening the buttocks) restricts movement, the technical advantages provided by these pelvic actions would appear to be somewhat different from what is often perceived.

As performers in any genre deal with far more than we can analyze in terms of mechanics, they frequently devise unique ways of getting the look and/or sound that they want. Whether or not there may be other ways to meet the same objectives is rich territory for research!

As regards resonance, tucking or tilting *can* change the sound of the voice and in the process, may provide a feeling of security for the singer/actor. Performers mention strength, support, and control of volume and texture. However, what additionally may be happening, for example, in the larynx and vocal tract, has yet to be investigated. We do know that engagement of pelvic floor muscles does not require backward tilt of the pelvis or gripping of the buttocks, although pelvic floor may well engage in the course of tilting or tucking.

References

Chapman, J. *Singing and Teaching Singing: A Holistic Approach to Classical Voice.* San Diego: Plural, 2006.

Curcio, R. Interview with Joan Melton, "Relating Voice and Dance Techniques." New York City. Also, Melton, J. (2011). Interview with Rusty Curcio. *Voiceprint 40*, Melbourne: Australian Voice Association, 2009.

Grieg, V. *Inside Ballet Technique: Separating Anatomical Fact from Fiction in the Ballet Class.* Heightstown, NJ: Dance Horizons, 1994.

Hixon, TJ. *Respiratory Function in Singing: A Primer for Singers and Singing Teachers.* Tucson: Reddington Brown, 2006.

Hodges, P. Melton, J. "Breath Management Strategies of Elite Vocal Performers across a Range of Performance Genres." Brisbane: University of Queensland, 2010.

McCoy, S. *Your Voice: An Inside View.* Princeton: Inside View Press, 2004.

Malde, M, Allen, MJ, Zeller, KA. *What Every Singer Needs to Know About the Body.* San Diego: Plural, 2009.

Melton, J. "Tucking the Pelvis: Actual and Perceived Outcomes." New York: Voice Theatre Solutions, 2011, www.joanmelton.com/articles.

PART III

Triple Threats
ON DANCING
WITH VOICE

7. Interview with Rin Allen

RIN ALLEN

Rin Allen is a New York-based American actress who grew up an expatriate in Southeast Asia and Western Europe. She holds a BFA in theatre from New York University and works in a wide range of media, from TV and film to panoramic theatre in the parks of New York City.

Rin and I met in 2013, when I was coaching and music directing a New York Classical Theatre production of Shakespeare's The Tempest *in Battery Park. Sean Hagerty, who directed the show, cast three terrific musical theatre performers in the part of Ariel, with Rin in the lead—for a composer, Rin is a gift! She has a superb ear, learns quickly, and is both imaginative and consistent. The following season, Rin played Rosalind in* As You Like It, *Stephen Burdman, director, in three outdoor venues: Central Park, Prospect Park (Brooklyn), and Battery Park.*

Mid-winter 2014, Rin and I got together at the National Opera Center in New York to record the following conversation:

JM: One comment I hear repeatedly is that breath is seldom mentioned in dance classes.

RA: Yes, that's true, that's true.

However, as you're also a singer and actor, I'm wondering what you're aware of, if anything, when you're dancing without voice, and are there differences when you're dancing and using voice at the same time?

I think there are, both in terms of my own awareness of breath and in terms of my own dance performance. The only teacher I've had that specifically addressed breath in depth during a dance class was Steven Sofia. He's since retired and moved to the west coast, but he was very adamant that our entire warm-up be very grounded, breathing-wise, and I found that in my last year of training in college, that made a big difference. Up until that point even in just an isolated dance class, not necessarily using the voice at all, I tended to hold tension across my shoulders and in my neck, which is the opposite of what I should be doing if I'm a dancer. I should be elongating the line, creating that profile for ballet and for jazz; yet that's where I seem to hold tension most often in my life because those are the muscles in my body that are the weakest. I have the least support there innately, and tend to crunch up. So having that groundedness become part of the warm-up—his actively walking around and poking you to see if you're breathing—that had never happened to me before. I noticed that when I danced in his classes, it changed my posture and my ability to express through dance, because suddenly the whole head-to-upper-chest region was looser and freer. And that was really cool.

I have to remind myself of that in dance. When I'm dancing with voice, I still tend to use an outward sort of push [in the abs] to maintain an even and well-placed sound, because what I'm doing in the dance might disrupt the stability of my voice—like for example, a couple of years ago I performed in the musical *Cats* in regional theatre, and that's a very active show.

Which cat were you?

I was one of the two sexy cats. I was Bombalurina, and it was nice that during the major duet [with Demeter] that we sang together, much of that dancing was sort of slow and slinky, and so I had to work less to sound decent. But the rest of the show has some very considerable dance breaks and there's also a lot of dancing and singing at the same time, whereas in a lot of musicals we have the step touch, step touch, sway from side to side, and then we have a dance break where we don't sing at the same time. For *Cats* I realized that much of my breathing had to come from my back because I was constantly using my abs. I think that show taught me a lot about breathing because I was both out of breath most of the time from the dance, and needed to be able to sing the second soprano line, which for me was relatively high.

Oh, yes, the sopranos go super high! It's interesting, what you just said: that during the duet you were being very slinky so didn't have to worry so much about the singing. Do you think the movement helped?

I think it did to a certain extent. I think the static poses—the low crouch, bent knees and the ability to open up the back—were incredibly helpful. I realized, as still sort of a younger performer, I had difficulty translating that groundedness to the very committed "Jellicle Ball," when you're singing and dancing at the same time and everything is "up" and the leaps are happening and the legs are flying in the air. So I was very grateful that the major sections that I sang by myself had that grounded, slow, slinky choreography. I was able to worry less about breathing deep and supporting because it happened naturally in those positions, whereas when everything in the choreography became in-and-up, my breathing did the same thing.

Do you think awareness of, or conscious use of pelvic floor muscles is ever part of the equation?

I think I'm less aware of that when I'm dancing. And in some ways I'm more conscious of it as a tightening than as a loosening because (a) I'm dancing, and (b) when I'm in a musical, particularly when it's very dance heavy, I'm constantly drinking water—all the time! For example, in that show I had two unitards on and I was onstage the whole time. So I could not use the bathroom at all until intermission. I was pounding water until places, and had to maintain that pelvic floor tension because I couldn't use the bathroom until halfway through the show! So for some natural reasons, in addition to, "Oh, yeah, I'm dancing," there was just like, "Don't let that go, don't let that go! It's not time yet!"

Wow! Interestingly enough, most of the research on pelvic floor has had to do with incontinence.

Oh, that's so funny.

What researchers have observed is that abdominal and pelvic floor muscles work together and in the same direction. So when the abs release for the in-breath, pelvic floor would normally release (or loosen) at the same time. I'm particularly interested—not necessarily from you, but from new research—in how much independence there is between abs and pelvic floor. Are they always working together to some extent, or can one work without the other? For example, when you were trying to keep from going to the bathroom, and you were engaging pelvic floor muscles all the time, could your abs have released?

I think I was very selective about when I released my abs. I think those muscles do work in tandem most of the time, so it needs to be a very conscious choice. But there were certainly higher notes that I had to hit in those songs, and I knew I was going to be pitchy if I was not breathing correctly for those. So I metered out a certain amount of control over that. When I could get away with keeping everything tight I allowed that because I felt much more comfortable performing that way. But in order to hit those high notes and to blend with other people, I chose selected moments to release.

That would seem to make sense. Though there are other questions on my list, I'd like to move on to outdoor theatre.

Ah yes!

The first show that you did outdoors was **The Tempest?**

Yes.

What conscious adjustments do you think you made, breath-wise, for that show, and later for **As You Like It,** *when you had, not a lot of singing, but a humongous amount of text? You were onstage nearly the whole show, and in challenging spaces: Central Park, Prospect Park, and Battery Park. So I'm wondering what your journey might have been from that first encounter with the space for* **Tempest** *through the changes that were required for* **As You Like It.**

Sure. *The Tempest* was my first engagement with unamplified outdoor theatre [Figure 7.1]. Since I was one of three Ariels and we split that role, both vocally and physically, I think in some ways that was a perfect form in which to explore a new environment. For a lot of the show, the movement for the three Ariels was very specifically choreographed so that our voices went directly to the audience, and we also spoke together with the same lines. So while it was certainly demanding to make that transition from film work and amplified musicals in an indoor space to a large, unamplified outdoor arena, I think I was able, to a certain extent, to lean on the other actors as I learned, because three voices together, once you actually get the diction at the same tempo, have more volume than just myself. I was aware that I had to deepen my breathing much more than I was used to for speech, and ultimately it became much closer to how I breathe when I sing.

The difference, I think, between *The Tempest* and *As You Like It* is that in *The Tempest* I was playing one third, essentially, of a sort of non-human, emotionally disconnected being that didn't require the same amount of elasticity or inflection or emotional injection as Rosalind.

When it came to *As You Like It*, I still had all of the mechanics that I remembered from *The Tempest*, but didn't initially have the vocal control. At first I didn't have the pitch control, I didn't have the fluidity of range, I didn't feel like I was connecting how I felt about any particular moment in a speech to how it was sounding. Although the mechanics existed, I hadn't been able to practice those mechanics with a very emotional moment, so managing to use that kind of volume and power and still inflect moments of tenderness and moments of light and joy without becoming brassy...That was very difficult and I remember during the rehearsal process you and I spent a lot of time working on which voices were lower and more masculine and more formidable, and when that light, flowery, young female side could come out, because until that point, most of my work in *The Tempest* had been that sort of androgynous, metered volume.

Creating a more nuanced voice for a much more nuanced character was both exciting and frustrating. "I know what I want to do with it. I just don't know how to make it happen! I'm squeezing in all the right places and it's just not working." I think ultimately we found a balance between the two: a much more nuanced speech pattern and vocal work, without compromising too much of the volume or diction. But it took the whole rehearsal period to make it happen. I'm hoping that soon I'll have a chance to apply that to some musical work, because it would be really interesting to see how that goes. I know that when I sing I'm usually the one that gets turned down on the mic in the sound system—like "Okay, we need less of Rin," because I tend to be very brassy and very loud when I sing. Whereas when I do straight plays, more often than not, I will get the opposite note. I have not done an indoor piece of theatre since *As You Like It*, so I'm really excited to see how I can translate everything I learned from that outdoor space to an indoor space.

You made a transition, there was a distinct difference when you finally had the voice that you needed...

So it could be heard everywhere!

Do you know what you did? Or did the body just figure it out?

I think it was sort of a combination of feedback and adjustments from you, and at the same time I think the body innately wants to find the easiest and most efficient way to do things. I feel like sometimes, when we only follow one specific kind of training, it makes it difficult for our bodies to let go of that training and find the easiest way. So for a while there I was fighting through: "I need to push out and I need to lock down and I need to use those muscular structures." Then at a certain point it became much more fluid and my body understood when those moments needed to happen, and when it could just exist in a sort of pre-structured vessel and the sound could echo around without necessarily being forced out of my body. A lot of that transition had to do with external notes, because in a space that large, I don't have an accurate concept of how I sound from the outside.

You can't.

When I'm in an indoor space, at least I can sort of hear a bounce-back off the chairs or the audience. Even in a full house you still get a little bit, and if you're mic'd at all, then you have the feedback from the monitors, whereas in an outdoor space, with less matter in front of you, there's really nothing to go off. I think that external feedback was incredibly important to the process.

I do think there's something to be said for your body, at a certain point, realizing that it's creating more work for itself than it needs to. But I feel like that can be said for really good acting as well; that at a certain point your body, if you've done the rehearsal process correctly, realizes that you don't need to force any of those moments, that if you're doing it right the work is there and it happens. It happens naturally, and it happens with emphasis at the right moments and nothing comes across as actor-intentioned or as forced. The audience should not look at you and say, "Ah, she's acting." But the audience also shouldn't look at you and go, "Ah, she's breathing right." It should be a normal process that comes as part of the language and as part of the moments that happen onstage. I think it took a while for my body to let go of "It's not quite right yet, not quite right yet," and just trust that that was going to happen.

Will you say a bit about your journey? You have lived a lot of different places in the world and you've trained in multiple directions. When did you begin as a performer, and did you start with dance?

I started as a dancer. My mom had done some tap dance and some jazz as a hobby, and I really liked that idea, so when I was probably three, two to three, I was put in dance classes and I loved it. Did that until, I would say, nine or 10. You know, we all go through a phase when we're like, "I don't like that anymore! I did that when I was a baby." So I took some time off from dance and began singing instead when I was 13 or 14, in school choirs. The middle school and high school that I went through had an arts curriculum requirement every year, and I'm terrible at drawing, so I'm like, "Oh, I'll be in the choir. That will be fun. I like that." And I really enjoyed it, and I started taking private voice lessons and I started singing in a women's quartet. And somewhere in that process, I think my freshman year of high school, there was an audition for the annual fall musical, so I auditioned for that and had a great time. I was like, "Oh, this is really fun. I forgot that I liked to dance." So I started dance again, ballet, jazz and modern, started doing pointe work a little bit, and continued all of those things, including theatrical work in the shows, through high school graduation. Decided that that's what I wanted to do in my life and went to college at NYU specifically for musical theatre. Obviously I went through the voice program, which was both voice technique, for which we had a class, and separate lessons. I took all of the dance classes, tap, ballet and jazz. We had voice and speech classes and regular scene study classes as well. So that was three and a half years. Then after I graduated I got into stage combat and the stunt world, which is worth mentioning because breath work is incredibly important in a very effective way. When you're translating the truth of violence, rather than the reality, a truth of violence onstage, what makes it more believable to an audience than anything else is hearing the reactions. Not so much an on-voice reaction, it's that [gasps], that sort of aspirated breath that does so much for translating the story. I find the violence work to be one of the ways I connect most deeply to an audience, because not everyone has experienced *love*. Not everyone has experienced the *loss* of someone yet, or *finding* someone…those are all things that, hopefully, we will experience as human beings. But everyone understands *pain*—everyone! So I find that to be an extremely vulnerable and touching connection to have with an audience. And translating that breath work into acting was a milestone for me.

What was the source of your training? It sounds very good indeed!

I really enjoyed it. I think, similar to dance and to voice work, not everything works for everyone. I was very fortunate in that the teacher I had was exactly what I needed. He recognized that as a dancer I learned choreography quickly. It was a matter of helping me put the pieces together: the acting work, the breath work and the actual choreography, all in one. I went through the Society of American Fight Directors, but more important personally to me than the organization was my individual teacher. I studied with David Brimmer almost the entire time, over the course of probably three years. We're still in touch and I still assist him on projects every now and then. He was so adamant about the breath work. It was more important to him that the breath work be there than that a punch read, because on any given night an actor might be in the wrong place onstage, or the actor you're working with may not be someone who's trustworthy about hitting that mark every given time. So you have to do everything in your power to make it believable, and the one thing that you can control is your own body onstage. He was so adamant about that and it made such a difference in my performance with stage combat, that I started applying that work to the fight work I did for film and the general stunt work that I've done in the non-union world, and it's made a huge difference in the performance quality. When

I reminded myself that I was more interested in acting than in just iso-lated fight work, I was like, "Well, I feel like I've learned so much from this that it would be stupid to just drop it. There's no reason this can't exist in my acting too." It's just a matter of using it intelligently and put-ting it in in bits and pieces.

One last question: do you have any advice for a young person who wants to go into theatre?

I think a lot of my light bulb moments have been a matter of stringing one art form into another, because when you rehearse something—when you're in school, or even when you're out in the professional world—you've gotten the job and you have blocking rehearsals. You have the rehearsal with the director for the big monologue in Act II, and you have the music rehearsals and the Sitzprobe, and you have the dance rehears-als. And it really isn't until you do the run through for the tech people and the designers that oh, wait, you're doing it all at the same time! And I feel like if I'd made a point of, not necessarily rehearsing them all at the same time because you don't always have control over that—unless you have really thick walls and a large living room, which you don't have in New York—I feel like just going through the music at home and putting the choreography with it in my brain and going, "Oh, that's the part where I'm doing a triple pirouette and the fan kick—note to self: rehearse that with those muscles in mind," would make translating it into a full sound when we hit the actual stage a lot easier.

And vice versa, taking more of the body into an audition, because I get stage fright. That sounds really stupid but I have really bad stage fright. And so going into auditions I have to fight against, "I'm just go-ing to stand in the center of the room and sound pretty and do acting with my eyes. I'll act really hard with my eyes and surely that will be enough." I know that's not enough, and that rehearsing those audition pieces without conveying anything with my body is pointless because I'm hoping to do it in a Broadway house. If I only want to do things in a tiny black box I can get away with tiny gestures and standing in one spot, but if I intend to be delivering it eventually to 900 people from the stage—in five years—then everything needs to be bigger. Not bigger in an overdone way, just bigger in a more communicative way. I feel like, for example, when I go into my lessons with my voice teacher, there's no reason I can't stretch while I'm doing my vocalises. There's no reason that I can't make that transition for myself. Taking ownership of that education, since no one else is really prepared to do it for you, has been vital, I think, to progression in my skill set.

Thank you so much, Rin!

Photographs

Headshot by Dechart Photography, Figure 7.1 by Miranda Arden for New York Classical Theatre, *The Tempest*, Sean Hagerty, Director, Battery Park, NYC 2013.

References

New York Classical Theatre, www.newyorkclassical.org, http://www.joanmelton.com/tempest, http://www.joanmelton.com/you-it.

Website: www.rinallen.com

8. Interview with Mara Davi

Mara Davi was my singing student at California State University Fullerton. She was also in my voice/movement classes and in productions that I coached. At her first lesson, I said, "You're a star," and in the middle of her second year she left CSUF to join the tour of 42nd Street.

Mara has done leads on Broadway, including Judy in Irving Berlin's White Christmas, *Janet in* The Drowsy Chaperone, *and Maggie in* A Chorus Line, *along with other New York performances, regional theatre, national tours, and TV. In 2012, she released a debut album, "Unspoken," with her band,* **Mara and the Bitter Suite.**

Late fall, 2014, Mara and I met at Pearl Studios, NYC, to talk about her journey to date as a performer and what it's like to deal technically with the demands of musical theatre performance.

JM: What came first: dance, singing, acting?

MD: My mother put me in ballet and tap combo classes when I was three years old, and at the same time I was obsessed with Disney movies. So I would say that I started dancing right away and I started singing by listening to *The Little Mermaid*. I stayed in dance class all through my childhood and I sang with my mom and my sister at church, and then when I was 10, I was an orphan in the musical *Annie*, and that's when I started doing community theatre: *Bye, Bye Birdie, 42nd Street, Joseph and the Amazing Technicolor Dreamcoat, My Fair Lady...*

Tell me about your mom. Is she a musician?

My mom has always sung, never professionally, but she sang in every church choir and in praise bands, and when she was a child she played guitar. In her high school musicals she was always shy, she didn't want to be in the spotlight, but she's always loved to sing so was in the ensemble. Later on, when my sister and I were doing community theatre my mom got roped in and played some leading roles. My sister and I got our singing chops from our mother.

And your sister is younger than you?

Two years.

You were taking tap and ballet...

And musical theatre and jazz...I drifted out of ballet, primarily stayed with tap dancing. And then came college and I got back into my dance training and I studied with you, so you know what my vocal training was like at that time.

Yes, you were coming from, "Do I do this in my head or my chest or…"

And you know, it's really interesting, I remember your saying at that time, "Voices change and it might just happen when you're near 30…" and at 28 my voice changed. Something happened and this new part of my voice that had kind of been lurking, developed. And so, that head voice that I had with you is still not as strong as I would like it to be, and it might even be weaker, because I found something stronger to take its place. I have my mix, but a mix that goes up to a [high] C, so I've just completely abandoned that other head voice.

I heard that when I came to the send-off of your CD.

Yes! It was actually working on that album when this new part of my voice developed. I was singing so close to a microphone that I was able to investigate some thinner fold sounds and then those thin folds grew more powerful.

When you were training early on, was anything ever said about breath in dance or voice—or were there conflicts?

It wasn't really mentioned when I was a kid…things were very separate. I took a musical theatre class—as a kid, they're worried about making sure you are hitting your mark, smiling big, and singing so your mom can hear…and you do it somehow. And I was a belter primarily, so I had that gusto. I took big breaths to get it out to the balcony. So it wasn't really until I was in your class in college that I started to think about how breath is related to movement, and especially something that still stays with me is the silent inhalation.

Oh yes.

I hear so many noisy inhalations from performers on stage and also, when I'm getting out of breath in a dance number I feel when I want to gasp. But I would say that in allowing the silent inhalation, the voice is more free. That is one of the most important things that stuck with me. I just think it makes a performance clearer and freer in every way.

Also, when I was getting ready to do *A Chorus Line* in college, I was studying jazz with Macarena [Gandarillas]. We would get done doing pushups and then she would make me sing the highest notes of "Music and the Mirror." And that sticks with me too. Pushups are the thing… they are the thing to get you warmed up, get your blood flowing, and if you can sing that note at the end of 10 – 20 pushups, then you build up that stamina.

I love that! I do jumping jacks, then pushups, then Shakespeare every morning.

Absolutely. Pushups are my favorite. And one of my other favorites, too—in my yoga class we call it the *Breath of Joy* [3-part breathing technique from Kripalu tradition]. If you do that for a while it opens the chest, gets the spine going, and everything just feels so open!

In research studies, we saw a* pattern *in which the deepest of the abdominal muscles, the transversus, engaged and released with the voice, regardless of physical position or activity. That would make sense because of its connection with the diaphragm.

However, some dance teachers say the most internal muscles need to remain engaged and if anything lets go it should be the outer muscles—for example, rectus abdominis. But studies have shown rectus to be relatively uninvolved in breath management.

So I'm wondering what you do when you are dancing without voice. Then is there something different that you consciously—or maybe unconsciously now—do when you begin to sing?

Hmm, it's really interesting, as a musical theatre performer it is so rare that you're doing fouetté turns, or something that requires intense center, all the transverse, its full engagement...the choreography is built so the steps are more simple when you're singing.

So from your experience, the choreographer does take into consideration what else you have to do.

Yes, I think in multiple ways: First of all, when you're singing, people want to see your face...I was just working with a choreographer recently who put steps wherever she could; however, they were in between the lyrics, so you'd sing a phrase and then do a double pirouette before you sing the next phrase. So breath control is more just about stamina than having to do both things at once. I've never had to sing something crazy while doing a pirouette or something like that. It wouldn't be enjoyable to watch.

Right. But I seem to recall that when you played Cassie in A Chorus Line *at Cal State Fullerton you had to do a cartwheel and come out of it singing a high A.*

That was probably *Dames at Sea* where I did the cartwheel, but in both of those shows, definitely there was a lot of aerobic activity, and then singing. In *A Chorus Line* she does 30 seconds of intense dancing and then holds a B or C for a very long time. But still, when the singing happens... well, no, now I remember that cartwheel, I was going [sings 8ve leaps to high A, then B flat]...

Yes!

I think, for myself personally, I'm not the best with my center as it is, so I think it does do that little bit of release [for inhalation], like you were saying, the release before...when you're doing a cartwheel it doesn't require full contraction, just enough [demonstrates].

One of the things I'm getting from you is that you've always put these things together, so whatever it is, you come at it with, "Okay, let's see, how do I do that?"

Yes, it's a give and take, I'd say, primarily an instinctual give and take where your body just knows I need a certain amount of energy for the physical exertion, for the dance, and I need a certain amount of power for the notes I'm singing, and I think that, to a certain extent, directors and choreographers do take it into account. They do want to challenge you, they want it to be exciting and thrilling, so they'll be like, "Work on this. We need your stamina up." But if it's your final preview and you're still out of breath, then maybe they'll say, "Let's simplify this. We want the story to be told."

That's good to hear...what you're saying sounds very sensible, as if everybody involved with the show wants it to be good.

In my experience, they care most about the telling of the story, the best way to tell the story, and if something is getting in the way...

Right. But I've heard tales from performers in various parts of the world about a lack of communication among artistic staff and performers who were left trying to do the impossible.

A couple of thoughts: I'm sure there are similar incidents to what you describe, but I've had only positive experiences thus far. My other thought is:

I've been fortunate enough to be a principal in every show that I've done. I do feel like there's a lot more demand on the ensemble members not to say, "No," not to say, "That step is too much for me to do while I'm singing," or "I can't sing that high note while doing that step." They're just told to do it. But when you're the lead in the show and you're in the spotlight, they're like, well, we want you to look good. We need you to look good.

When it comes to challenges in the ensemble— to juggle and spin and sing high A at the same time—I think sometimes people just settle for not the most beautiful, supported high A. They compromise. You have three people all singing that note, so it will be covered.

On the other topic about the requirement for muscle contraction and holding center while dancing, I do feel like in performance there is that ebb and flow, tension and release, and when you are in this flow, performance feels glorious. I think things like that *Breath of Joy* and other flowing, spinal twisting movements are so helpful to get that instinctual body…There are times when I'll be in a very emotional scene— and any time I feel like I'm pushing to get something out—I feel a very visceral need to [demonstrates subtle movement in the upper back and neck]…find some way to release gripping muscles…okay, if I can just roll through my spine and twist to one side just a little bit, often the emotion will be unlocked. That happened at this audition today. The emotions were there but then I was gripping. So all I did was a breath and…release.

Amazing how the body informs the emotion, an outside-in approach.

The outside-in approach is often very effective for me.

Was there ever any confusion around breath management, from one class to another, from one technique to another?

Oh, sure, I've never been able to subscribe to that operatic "hold your ribs at a certain size."

Yes, holding the ribs out seems counter to what you'd be doing as a dancer. Another technique that quite a few musical theatre performers encounter is the **down** *and* **out** *method of breath management, pushing down with the abs during voicing.*

I've heard of that but I don't even know…

No worry, that too would be contradictory.

I would say there's something that I still…I get confused about and I don't know, I think there's a compromise that has to be made when you're dancing…the yogic breath. Complete lower belly release is not something that you can do to its full extent when you're holding your abs in for centering, so I find again doing those pushups and doing the Breath of Joy tends to expand the ribs and open up the chest. I'd say that is the most helpful for me. Also, I practice holding the lower abs in and still trying to find the breath that you can stretch within that, trying to find more space in the lower back and sides.

What about pelvic floor, any awareness?

Not that much that I can think of. I do have awareness of it when I'm in class for dance or for yoga, but then when I get to the show it's like, okay, what's going to get the job done? I am interested in engaging it when I'm just exploring it, especially on an exhalation in Ujjayi breathing, but I feel like it locks me up to try to do that in performance…when I focus on the pelvic floor, I suddenly can't focus on anything else.

Do you have any advice for young dancers looking for a career in musical theatre?

Yes, I think my advice would be: you have to be well rounded. You can't just dance. You have to sing and you have to act, and the better you do all three, the better you're going to do and the more longevity you're going to have. Fortunately for dancers in musical theatre—a Broadway dancer's career used to be done by 30, but now, I have friends who are 50 and fabulous and dancing. However, most of those friends are also good actors and singers so they are playing principal and supporting roles.

With regards to what we were talking about earlier, definitely trust yourself, trust that you can sing, find what you like to sing. If you want to be in musical theatre don't define yourself as a dancer. I've lived a life of saying that I'm equal at all three, Jack of all trades/master of none. I've had my struggles in each of them but…have confidence and really, really study singing, study acting so that you're not coming to the big city with unnecessary insecurities…I just talk to so many dancers who say, "I can't sing" and it breaks my heart. When you're young, if you can, study so you don't have to worry about that…You don't want to worry about those things, you just want to be able to start getting a job and telling a story.

I don't want to be defined as a dancer. I dance. My main advice is: study, but don't study in fear, study in enjoyment. Find who you are, find what defines you. And also, for dancers in the ensemble, yes, there is unity, yes, you do need to meld into the group, but I think that a lot of training…when people are training chorus members, they're taking the individuality out of people and that really concerns me. I feel like it's happening at a lot of colleges where they're like, "Your way into show business is going to be in the ensemble, so you all need to learn how to do your hair the same, and dress the same, and sing all of these styles the same way." And yes I do think the more range that you have, the better. But know who *you* are. There was so much time where I was trying to be this lyric soprano and this dramatic mezzo because, type-wise, as an actor I could fit into that, but I didn't feel authentic, and when finally I was just able to focus on the things that I was really good at and feel ownership of those things, then I was able to thrive. The shows that I was getting to do…I wasn't showing up at the theatre worried about whether I was capable of doing it or not. I got to come and do my job, whereas when I was trying to fit my square peg in a round hole or vice versa, then every day was like, "Oh, my gosh, am I going to make it through the show today? Am I going to be able to sing that note?" When I was finally doing shows where I was like, "Wow, this role was written perfectly for me," then I thought, "Great, now I just get to tell the story."

It is hard because you want to get a job, you want to be everything to all people, but just keep striving to find who you are and what you really have to say, and hopefully people want *that.*

You left school in the middle of your sophomore year to do the tour of 42nd Street, so how did you continue to study, especially acting, when you were no longer in a program? Obviously it's been the best thing for you.

Yes, it's been wonderful, especially living in New York. You can pick and choose your teachers. When I first got to New York City I went to Terry Schreiber's studio for three months, taking a scene study class and a monologue workshop. Then when I was on Broadway doing *A Chorus Line* and *Drowsy Chaperone* I was too busy, I wasn't in class. And then after I got married I suddenly went through a dry spell, and also I wasn't 22 anymore getting by on my sweetness—I realized, oh, you're growing up, you need to act like a leading lady. So I was in scene study class and did private coaching with Joan Rosenfels for a year and then in 2010 I started studying with Rob McCaskill, where I'm going tonight. I've stuck with him for a very long time. He is my home base, and I love having a safe place where I know I can continue to grow. I also go to other classes for a little comedy and improv. I've studied at the UCB [Improvisational and Sketch Comedy Training Center]. For voice, I studied with Jane Kennedy and then with Tom Burke. I haven't taken voice a lesson in a very long time.

You sounded wonderful a few minutes ago!

So you go through times of learning when you're not doing a show.

Mara, you're fantastic and I thank you very much!

Photograph

Headshot by Murphy Made Photography

References

Breath of Joy, https://yogainternational.com/article/view/breath-of-joy.

Website: www.maradavi.com

9. Interview with John Robert Armstrong

John Robert Armstrong is an actor, director, and teacher of a wide range of performance subjects. He holds a BA in musical theatre and an MFA in acting from Indiana University (IU), has taught at IU, Indiana Repertory Theatre, Cleveland Playhouse, Paper Mill Playhouse, and was on the acting and musical theatre faculty at Ohio Northern University for five years. Professional acting and directing credits include Off Broadway, regional theatre, national tours, and film. He is associate producer of Pigasus Pictures, LLC, and on the teaching faculty of New York Film Academy.

John played Touchstone in New York Classical Theatre's 2014 production of As You Like It and served brilliantly as music and dance captain for the show. I had the pleasure of working with him on that production.

Early January 2015 we got together at Pearl Studios, NYC, to talk about acting, voice, dance and the multidimensional performer.

JM: You are at Paper Mill?

JA: Yes, Paper Mill Playhouse in Millburn, NJ. They have a huge education program, and a summer conservatory where I've taught, musical theatre based.

So you've been with them before. This is not new.

No, the college prep program is new this year. I developed it with two other teachers on the education staff. I have 10 private students that I'm helping to advise, gather material for, and prep for auditions…now you have to perform a pre-screen video to send to a college before you can audition in person. I coach them on songs and monologues, putting a package together, and help them get into college. I enjoy that work a lot.

It's really hard. Kids don't know one school from another, there are so many programs now, it's very competitive, and very commercial. So we help navigate young people through that process.

I'm sure you're doing a great job. From what I observed during the summer [As You Like It], you're an excellent teacher.

Well, I love the balance. Love to perform, but I don't like to struggle to perform. When I have auditions from my representation I go, but I'm not desperate to get that job.

When did you begin as a performer and what came first in your training: dance, voice, acting?

Acting was first—which is funny because I would say singer first, but I guess if we talk about the 3rd grade, I did a play, loved the play, then sometime later I did community theatre, and then as a 6th grader I was cast in the high school musical. They were doing *Bye, Bye Birdie*, needed a little Randolph MacAfee and the elementary school choir director said, "Here's a young kid who can sing." I always sang in choir and when I got into theatre it was ultimately through music.

And where was this?

In Brownsburg, Indiana. She just retired, Deborah Prather, wonderful choir director, singer and pianist. She taught me to love music. Working with her was an emotional experience. I did musicals at the same time and did a couple of plays in high school.

Did you study dance in high school or earlier?

In high school, in the show choir we danced our faces off. It was more about…I didn't learn technique, I didn't know ballet positions or how to turn. It was basic jazz dance but really about precision, clean movement, unified dance, and emotion. It wasn't till college that I studied dance.

The first year of college was kind of exploratory. I was taking voice lessons because I took voice lessons through high school and learned that singing was the thing I liked. So I took lessons from a graduate student at Indiana University, Darin Adams, now a voice teacher in the city and still a wonderful friend. I applied to one school, went there for psychology, took these voice lessons, and this wonderful teacher said, "You know, if you want to make a go of this, I think you could get into music school." I said, "Okay." I was a first generation college student, so as long as I was in college my parents didn't care what I was doing and I realized that academics weren't my forte at that time.

So I auditioned, got into music school, transferred to a faculty voice teacher, Michael Belnap, still classical singing—and belt, he had a lot of musical theatre students. Then after about a year and a half, once music theory got to a point that I was like, "I'm not happy doing this," I was taking a ballet class. That was one of my first dance classes and a guy in that class said, "I'm a musical theatre major." And I said, "What is that?" He said, "You know, you do musicals." And I said, "Oh, that's what I like." Back then—this is 1997—there wasn't this boom of musical theatre schools, so it was kind of a new concept. So I went to the Theatre Department, talked to the head of the musical theatre program, George Pinney, who's still a friend and mentor, auditioned for him and he took me on. So I made the transfer to the Theatre Department, but stayed with my faculty voice teacher in the music school all through undergraduate because I wanted to have good, solid singing technique.

Through my music theatre program I had to take a lot of dance: ballet almost every semester, jazz and tap. I never took modern. Violette Verdy was head of the ballet program, so it was a very prestigious program and the training was very good. I was always a coordinated person so took to dance very fast. I had a good center, was able to turn and came along pretty quickly. So that was musical theatre.

As I continued on, I really liked the acting portion but it wasn't my focus. Graduated from school, came to New York, did some regional musical theatre and the national tour of *Seussical the Musical*.

What did you play?

Wickersham brother. I was the Cat in the Hat's understudy. The other two Wickersham brothers were two friends of mine from college. The three of us got cast together and had a wonderful time.

I knew I wanted to go to graduate school because I felt there was a better way to go about a career and I wanted to train more in acting. So I started visiting schools around the country, and while I was on tour my wife and I—I was married at the time—got pregnant and it was like, "I need to go to grad school *now!*" The next stop was Indiana and we were playing Indiana University, which was a fun homecoming for us three Hoosiers. It just so happened that the Theatre Department was holding on-campus MFA auditions the same weekend we were there. I had come from music school/musical theatre, so knew the acting teachers and we had good relationships, but I had never been in straight theatre. I auditioned and got in, so left New York, had a baby, started grad school three weeks later, and went to grad school to focus on acting. That's when—I'm taking from your book talking about this—there were three different things that I did: dancing, singing and acting, and once I started training as an actor I started to realize that this is all one thing.

Yes!

I had to learn how to breathe in acting school. I was already a singer but I had to learn how to breathe. It was like everything moved *down*. All about resonance and placement in music school. My voice teacher—amazing teacher, studied with Giorgio Tozzi, finalist in the International Pavarotti competition—also played piano, and from behind the piano could see me about there [chest up]. And he would just listen and look at my placement, my face and neck and jaw, and didn't talk much about what's happening down below. I think great singers with great support probably take it for granted. So breathing came along during graduate school and that's something that I continue to explore on my own. The work that we did last summer was really, really helpful. It gave me more concrete things to latch onto.

In As You Like It *[Figure 9.1] you had to make some specific adjust-ments from a mic'd sound indoors to an unmic'd sound out of doors. Can you describe technically what those adjustments were? For exam-ple, when I would come to a scene and say, "It's all too high, you've got to get it down," you said you knew what to do—one of the things I've learned over time is that not everybody does the same thing. So what* **did** *you do?*

At first, someone with technique pridefully says, "What's wrong with what I'm doing?" But I felt it, what you were saying. In a closed en-vironment you're used to sound coming back to you--that's the big difference. I remember I played Guido Contini [*Nine*] my last year in graduate school, which is a very vocally demanding role, and we'd do sound check. They leveled our mics, did sound check before the show, but during the performance the levels weren't right sometimes and I freaked out to the sound designer because it was like, if these levels aren't right I can't do the last number in the show because I can't hear myself. I would compensate for not being able to hear by pushing, and by the time I got to the big final number, I was fried. So, it's a real crutch, hearing yourself. Then as I started teaching, I started thinking about listening to how it feels and not how it sounds, so that idea came to me. But I'd never worked outdoors, and there, there's nothing coming back to you.

So I felt like, I'm out in the open, I don't know what to do, I can't listen to myself anymore, and that's when listening to how it *felt* really came into place. I was just so grateful that you were there. You kept saying, "It doesn't have feet." I was trying to get the breath low to feel support and I would get there sometimes. It wasn't solid but I realized I needed to stop pushing. In order to send sound out, for me it was always about placement—if you place things high, front, forward, and ping, you're going to resonate, so that's what I tried to do—like everything gets up here [demonstrates loud, bright sound]. That's the belt sensation from singing in music school, but there's nothing happening down low. Maybe I'm being heard, but nobody can understand a word I'm saying. So you would say it doesn't have feet and I would think, "I know exactly what she means, but…"

And you managed to open up the sound. Can you describe what you did or show me?

Sure, I did some workshops with Patsy Rodenburg so it kind of comes from that. First step is to release physical and psychological tension, and then I'd do yoga and try to stretch the ribs. I'd do the side stretch and the solar plexus. I'd do some *port de bras* across the front of the chest, then concentrate on the back of the lungs, the back of the chest. And then I'd start to work it down the back with a deep squat, deep plié, and then I'd get down to deep prayer squat and really try to get my breath down to sphincter…

Of course, we know breath is only in the lungs, but you're right, abdominal and pelvic floor muscles are our remote, and when you get into a squat all the action moves to the bottom of the torso.

Then I'd do breath exercises that don't have voice, like /sh/, I'd flutter the lips just to activate the support, abs working in and up, then slowly add sound, soft sounds. Lately what I do that's really helping my students is that I have them imagine they're tasting food, chewing and humming, and they say, "mmm." And then I tell them it gets better and better and they start going "mmm" [using more upper range and inflection]. Then we work down. You take something like a decadent food and start going to a nice deep, low sound, the feeling of a good hug, then down to the "om," a personal vibration. Everything works better with imagery—as long as you know the intention of the imagery—and as you go down, you feel more and more air expulsion.

Very interesting, what you're saying, John. During the ultrasound project in London, I was surprised that when I was really low in pitch I was using more breath.

I always equate it to brass instruments. If you're playing a tuba…

Do you play brass instruments?

No, but you can hear that, I think it's the same action. You can connect low in the body even on high pitches—that's what I was doing wrong, and I've seen tenors do this. As they get higher and higher and higher they start to top up [with breath], and they can get these really high notes but, as you said, no feet.

And in some circumstances they can get by with that, but not outdoors. We could hear you, but it wasn't a complete human being.

No, you were hearing part of an instrument. And as we worked on, two things really stuck with me and helped: In your office we started doing some yoga with sound. I remember we were doing upward dog, opening the throat with deeper sound, as well as downward dog with high sounds, and I really liked that. That's when I started thinking about this low thing. Then when I worked with Jennie [Morton], she started talking about the psoas muscle and how the arches of the feet relate to alignment of the pelvis and positioning of the psoas. And since the psoas connects to the diaphragm, this relates to breathing. So as I began to work to activate low support, I literally began to think about the psoas muscle and to explore [via tilting the pelvis] its range from being too tight, so it's not able to move, to being disengaged so it's like a loose rubber band. That was when we were in Battery Park, so the last leg of the show…

Also you helped me a lot with the speech—which I thought I kind of understood, but there was a cadence to the pentameter that I didn't quite understand—and that helped with breathing, rhythm.

Right.

This is a last question and it's particularly applicable to you because you're a teacher too and you've worked in a variety of media. Do you have advice for young performers, especially dancers or musical theatre performers, who want to have career options across genres?

About technique?

Yes, about technique, or attitude, when to train, what to train…

Recently I've been exploring chakra a lot, and what I've been reading has given me another way to articulate this kind of thing. There are two currents to a chakra energy flow. The downward current is called *manifestation*. It's the flow of energy we enact when we want to ground ourselves.

It's about being right here, getting out of your head and into your body, *manifesting* ideas into reality. The upward flow of energy is called *liberation*, the feeling of release, of letting go, of connection to the universe, upward, outward and beyond you. Taking what you have and *liberating* yourself from it.

I think that speaks to the balance that is important to performance. You can't let go till you ground yourself. The first half is preparation; there's a difference between preparation and performance. Students need to understand that when they're rehearsing or practicing, it's preparation, it's about opening everything up and taking it all in, not trying to do too much, but trying to listen, trying to drop in, bring your breath in, to internalize and be present. And then when it's time to perform, you work the other way and start to let it out, the same way the breath itself goes in and out. Preparation versus Performance, you have to acquire it before you can let it go. Young people try to perform before they're really ready. Then, as teachers, we have to go backward and fill in the blanks. I'm very meticulous when I teach, about *growing* a monologue or song…we don't perform and then work backwards.

The other thing is: We say that acting is living truthfully under imaginary circumstance in a beautifully artistic form. I've seen pop singers that are bad actors—Michael Jackson, amazing actor! Living truthfully in his form. You've seen dancers who are bad actors, and some actors are bad actors. So this definition of acting is about connecting. You can't just be a technician either. It's not creative until you live truthfully under whatever circumstances you've set up, and in that regard, all acting is the same. I have students right now who think acting is the stuff you do between songs in a musical. "Oh, those are the lines." "Oh, I'm not acting now, I'm dancing." It's all acting, and it's all one instrument.

I teach my students to stretch and warm up their voices and so they'll go to auditions and start stretching and people ask them, "Are we dancing today?"—because they're stretching, getting ready to *sing*. As you say, we have one instrument that needs to be available to us. Even if you're sitting in a chair like we are now, your breath has to be dropped down. So when I'm teaching at the film academy I have a voice and movement class in which there's no camera, we're just working with the instrument, and they take that [work] to their film class and go, "Yeah, I do need that." Especially under pressure, with all that stimulation around you, you have to ground yourself.

The next stage of my personal research or training is going to be in chakra meditation. I got started with Patsy Rodenburg's book, *The Right to Speak*. Love *The Right to Speak*, taught from it. In the chakra system—the seven major chakras—each has a different right. The root chakra is your right to *be here*. The first thing to tell yourself is, "I have a right to be here." The next one is your right to *feel*, I have a right to feel whatever I'm feeling. The solar plexus is the right to *act*. I'm able to follow my instincts, everything happens from the core. The heart chakra is my right to *love*, throat is my right to *speak*, third eye is my right to *see* clearly, and crown is my right to *know*. So it's not just the right to speak. There are seven main human rights, and the emotions we have register in these places. There is a reason why we feel the "pang of love" in the chest and feel "just sick about it" when we're guilty, and why our head goes, "Aha!" when we've had a revelation. And it's not a metaphysical, mystical experience. Modern science is getting onboard, and new research is showing that there is a physical basis for the idea of chakra, that it's all part of our nervous system. A book I've been reading I recommend: It's called *Eastern Body, Western Mind.*

I must get it!

It's basically taking Eastern philosophy and putting it into Western theory. So when actors say, "I want to connect," *where* do I want to connect? It's like a vast, blank sea, and you say, "Is this character having an awakening? Connect to that idea, in the head; be open-minded." Or have they been wronged, or someone that they love has been wronged, do they want to fight for that? That's going to come from the solar plexus, the burn in the belly. It takes the mystery out of *connection*. I really find it wonderful. The book also explains chakras as holes on a flute. Some need to be opened; some need to be held. So it's a matter of going through the chakras and saying, "Is this something I need to pay attention to?" Is it too open or too closed? Like your heart, it's about relationships. If all my energy is going out to others, that's when I become co-dependent and need to balance the chakra with more self-love. People who live in their head, people who live in theory and don't do practice—you need to turn theory into practice to *manifest* it—you say, "Hang on, hold that chakra for a second and come back to the world."

This is not just about acting. It's about life!

I would say there's no difference between who you are as a person and who you are as a performer. You need balance in your life in order to have balance as a performer.

If you're a niche performer, you got a great character type, you don't need a vast range of ability, you don't need to be a versatile performer. You got a thing that you're doing? Ride that thing to the bank! But if you're an actor in training who wants to do theatre, dance, musical theatre, TV, film, classical, contemporary, be marketable and versatile, then you have to explore the whole thing.

You may wind up focusing on one area, but you need to explore.

One informs the other. Being able to play Touchstone [*As You Like It*]—tell me my jazz and ballet classes weren't vital to the physicalization of the character. I was good at dance, I did it because it was part of musical theatre, it wasn't my medium, it wasn't my heart. But I find that when I do high comedy, I understand my character, the postures and positions, and I'm able to do that because I took those dance classes. So even though I did focus on one thing [acting] eventually…

The rest of it is there to support.

You never know, and New York Film Academy gets that. They have Shakespeare classes for film actors. Even in voice class for film actors— some of them have almost no experience, some of them have a lot, some of them none—I have to explain to them why Shakespeare and voice work are important—"I'm on camera, I don't have to project"—that's their idea.

There's more to it than that!

There's a lot more to it than that. And if you want to work, Shakespeare is still the most widely produced playwright on the globe. It's about versatility, being able to do anything. So I guess you can say I'm a triple threat.

Well, multiple threat…

You have to find *your* triple threat. It's not about being a singer, actor, dancer, not any more. That mentality produced a lot of great chorus people for a long time…back in the day there were so many iconic actors on the stage, and now there are far fewer up there. The last 20 years of training in musical theatre has been sing, act, dance, Jack of all trades, and a master of none. So if you have two left feet, you cannot dance and you'll never be in the chorus of a show, get some skills, get connected to your body, but go learn how to juggle, take puppetry, get another skill set. Do you play an instrument? If you can sing, act and play an instrument—you can't dance to save your life—you need movement, you need to be connected to your body, but after a certain point you're wasting your time in dance classes. That's how I felt about music theory, because I'm not a musician. I'm a singer and an actor, but once I got to drop the needle tests—you tell us the composer, movement and—I realized music school wasn't my thing, don't want to waste time because college is expensive! And these kids need to make the best use of their time.

A lot of programs are just: you need this, this, this. This is the degree, this is what you'll take every single semester, there's no deviation.

But every performer is unique.

They need a chance to find things out. I went to college as a psych major, then music school, I took some dance and found musical theatre. You can't do that anymore. These kids have to decide at age 17 or 18 if they want to be an actor, and they have to go through someone like me to get into a program that's going to help them do that. You can't go to college and explore anymore. You could, but it's gonna cost you $40,000 a year and you may not be accepted into a "TOP" program if you tell them you're not really sure what you want to do yet, you want to explore. That's why I say to these young people, "Hey, guys, it's not Broadway or bust. We're gonna figure out what you want to do, see where your heart goes, and find a program that will help you accomplish that."

This has been so helpful, John. Thank you again!

Photographs

Headshot by Emily Lambert, Figure 9.1 by Miranda Arden for New York Classical Theatre, *As You Like It*, Stephen Burdman, Director, Central Park, NYC 2014.

References

Judith, A. *Eastern Body Western Mind: Psychology and the Chakra System as a Path to the Self.* Berkeley: Celestial Arts, 2004.

Rodenburg, P. *The Right to Speak.* London: Methuen Drama, 1992.

PART IV

Research
IN MOTION

10. Practical Cats & a Laban Approach to Characterization

During March and April of 2015, I had the rare opportunity to work in a theatre program that offers a wide range of dance classes, individual singing lessons, classes in acting, voice, speech and dialects, and movement classes based in the Laban/Bartenieff System of Movement Studies.

Rusty Curcio (see Chapter 1), Head of Dance at Wagner College, was directing and choreographing *Cats*, which was an ideal production for truly integrating every aspect of the actor's work. I was brought onboard to help facilitate connections across trainings so that the actors were not dealing with this and that, but with a synthesis of performance elements that told a story.

> Everything informs the other, and if one piece is missing, then the others are weakened. (Joshua Sottile, Munkustrap)

Once the show opened I was able to interview several of the actors about the rehearsal process, which had opened new doors for some and challenged others in surprising ways.

Distinct themes emerged around breath management, phrasing of text, and the relation of voice and dance, for example:

> I think one of the things that saved my voice in the show was connecting from the consonants into the vowels. (Lisa Jeanne Peterson, Bombalurina)

I found a new strength with singing and dancing together. Incorporating the two of them I just felt a lot more open and free. (Clint Thompson, Plato/ Mr. Mistofelees swing)

When I started taking voice lessons my teacher could tell immediately if I came from dance classes because of the bad sound that was coming out. But recently he's said, "Whatever's been going on at *Cats,* keep it up." Now the days when I have the harder lessons are when I don't have dance, because this show has forced me to figure out how it all works together. (Jason Rath, Rum Tum Tugger)

Many of the actors came in with relatively high breathing patterns, audible inhalations, and little connection to the text. However, use of a Standard American for most of the cats, Standard British for Bustopher Jones, and vaudeville Brooklyn for Mungojerrie and Rumpleteazer helped to focus attention on the story and the physicality and hierarchy of the characters. The choreography throughout informed the vocal sound, and the rhythms of speech made patter songs a breeze.

When I was dancing and singing at the same time, my sound increased and was bigger and bolder than when I was still. (Addi Berry, Rumpleteazer swing/pit singer)

Once I had the movement I was able to incorporate the voice and dialect and it made sense. (TJ Lamando, Skimbleshanks)

Quite often with singing, the sound itself is the main attraction, but in the context of a show, *voice*—singing, speaking, meowing, hissing—serves a larger purpose, which can be both revealing and freeing for the actor.

I had to remember that you aren't just saying something because it's your line; you're saying it to tell the story. (Alec Reiss, Tantomile)

I'm a lyric soprano and "Macavity" was a challenge. But looking at it as speaking rather than singing helped me find that brassy sound and the placement that I needed. (Lisa Jeanne Peterson, Bombalurina)

In a show that has been done by signature singers, it is tempting to imitate or to think one must imitate those singers. This show was no exception, but the actors found out rather quickly that that was not where this production was going.

> Letting your body make the sound can be a little scary at first. You're like, whoa, where did that come from? But you have to love not sounding like every other girl in the line. Embrace what you have! (Maggie Marino Pitts, Co- Choreographer)
>
> [This process] helped me explore the range and richness in my voice that I never knew I had. (Nicole Amato, Sillabub)

While individual actors dealt with a range of challenges, many had common technical concerns. And the linchpin was breath management.

> Having to produce sound that could be heard from the back of the house while I was jumping or whatever was difficult at first. I wasn't sure how to go about it, but once I figured out how to breathe for both it got a lot easier. (Addi Berry, Rumpleteazer swing)
>
> You said, "Your body works this way naturally. You don't need to think about breathing in, because your body will breathe for you." So once I relaxed and stopped thinking about it, it was just like a machine working to produce the proper outcome. (Sydni Session, Cassandra/Bombalurina swing)

Discovering that the body can handle the in-breath without our attention was major, as was moving the action of "support" to the bottom of the torso.

> Not staying too lifted was really important because that made me lock up from the rib cage. That's where the breath was losing its control, so once I engaged in my lower half, it just opened it up for me. (Clint Thompson, Plato)

Efficiency was the key, which meant letting go of anything that wasn't essential. Breathing methods for singing are often taught in the context of stillness and of a standing body. But these actors were crouching, crawling, leaping and dancing for two and a half hours, so ordinary singer instructions had to be rethought.

At the same time, head/neck alignment was critical, both for voice production and for characterization. Demeter, for example, moved her head as part of the choreography, but when she was also singing she was careful to line things up:

> The choreography for this is always the head, but I kinda told myself just for those moments [in "Macavity"], don't do the neck because it would throw my voice off. So keep my head in line and maybe do more arm, or maybe do more with my hips, as opposed to the head. (Maria Salerno, Demeter)

Bustopher Jones initially lifted his chin, thinking it made him appear more confident—what Patsy Rodenburg would call "bluff." Then he realized that that worked against him, both as the "Cat about Town" and as a cat who sings!

In this and in most other productions, what I am looking for is clear, efficiently produced, ringing sound appropriate to the style, in any position, moving or still. And I expect to understand everything that is spoken or sung.

However, as with any other show, the director's vision trumps, so I asked Rusty Curcio what he expected vocally from the actors:

> I wanted them to be able to do it all, not to have to sacrifice one thing for the other. What I've been told in the past is that singers can't do their technique while they're moving, so I'm asked to sacrifice the movement.
>
> I brought you onboard because I knew you would listen when I said what's important at that moment, and that you had enough tools to find a way to make it work without sacrificing something else.

My concern had been that the vocal work might have a negative effect on the dance, since I was asking the actors to release the abs slightly for inhalation. So I questioned one of the lead dancers about this. His answer—and comments from others in the cast—indicated that they could indeed do it all:

> Through the vocal work I was able to free a lot of my movement as well, because I have habits of locking up and tensing muscles. Finding that freedom vocally helped me find it physically…so it was great. (Clint Thompson, Plato/Mr. Mistofelees swing)

Rusty corroborated this view:

> When I teach—even classical ballet classes—I have the students count very often, or I have them say the steps or recite poems while we're doing allegro work. It's not so much that they're developing their vocal skills, but it's releasing something that they're holding in their body, which allows them to feel more grounded and feel more weight. You can't dance until you feel your weight. Ballet dancing is an illusion that you don't have weight. But you are weighted, you have to be, because you can't jump unless you can push down. So many dancers think, "I'm not supposed to feel my weight," and that's why they're rise, rise, rising, and then they can't move fast, and then they also have more injuries. So by speaking, they drop their weight.

The Laban Approach

Having observed much of the process of character development, which began even in callbacks, I asked Rusty to talk about the benefits of Laban Movement Analysis (LMA) as an approach to characterization.

> There are two sides to it: The LMA training honed my eye and my ability to see what is truly there and figure out what is the *cause*, as opposed to what is the *symptom* of the expression. So I use that to direct and guide the actors through their process of character development. The training also gave me a stronger understanding of physical communication and the ability to use that for creativity and storytelling.

What it did for the actors was give them tools to build that physical style. Especially with a show like *Cats*, they can get caught up mimicking cats. It becomes mimicry. But because of all of the exploration work we did early on, they embodied the physicality and movement. From there we built the convention of the play and the world of the play, and they felt that embodiment as a place of safety, or comfort, instead of as a place of mystery or uncertainty. And once they feel that, anything can work onstage.

LMA puts movement into a non-technical place. It is technical but in their minds it's not technical because it's about expression. It's not about a tendu or a pirouette.

Hence, paired with the actor's imagination, the Laban approach allowed these practical cats to "feel" their scapulae turning from the vertical plane to the sagittal plane, as their arms functioned like cat limbs, and the specifics of *their* cat emerged [Figure 10.1].

Summary and Discussion

Late 2014, Rusty Curcio and I began discussing a project that would compare the breathing patterns of performers while dancing and while dancing with voice, using tasks from musical theatre and language from Laban Movement Analysis.

Then the opportunity to do a dance show that was also voice heavy appeared in the form of *Cats*. After working through what became the ideal performance-based project, we then took stock of what we'd learned, what remained to be investigated, and possibilities for future work.

Topping the list of what we learned was that it *is* possible for performers to do it all—acting, dancing, speaking, moving, singing—without sacrificing anything, and while remaining healthy. In addition:

1. Laban Movement Analysis served as an ideal approach to characterization.
2. Essential to synthesizing performance elements were:

   • Efficient breath management
   • Clear phrasing of text, including use of operative words, seeing the lines through, breathing with the thoughts, and breathing as often as possible
   • Consistent integration of voice/movement elements throughout the rehearsal process

What remains to be investigated are the specifics of individual patterns of breath management, as performers respond in unique ways to physical/vocal demands. In addition, it would be highly valuable to do a similar project (or projects) with actors from different backgrounds and in other settings.

Possibilities for future work include other performance, rather than lab-based, projects, since: (1) equipment for monitoring physical/vocal activity during extended movement is still extremely limited; (2) actual, rather than simulated, performance is the ideal laboratory; and (3) New York City is rich with opportunities for performance-based studies.

Photograph

Figure 10.1 by Phill Hickox

References

Lloyd Webber, A, Eliot, TS. *Cats,* musical based on *Old Possum's Book of Practical Cats* by TS Eliot (1939), with additional lyrics by Trevor Nunn and Richard Stilgoe. London: Premiere 11 May 1981, New London Theatre, Produced by Cameron Mackintosh, Trevor Nunn, Director, Gillian Lynne, Choreographer.

Melton, J. "Discussions with artistic staff and interviews with individual actors." New York: Wagner College, April/May 2015.

_____. "Conversations with Director/Choreographer Rusty Curcio." New York, May 2015.

Rodenburg, P. *The Actor Speaks: Voice and the Performer.* London: Methuen Drama, 1997, 31 – 33.

11. Widening the Lens

As the technical demands of theatre performance continue to cross disciplines, compartmentalized trainings become less efficient and the practitioner who is able to cross boundaries is highly valued.

"Widening the lens" starts with allowing our own boundaries to soften, or even crumble, so that we really *listen* to the rest of the artistic team and acknowledge that there are likely more variables than absolutes in what we do.

Coming from the part of this that I know best, *voice* in all its roles, dissolving instead of erecting artificial separations of this single instrument would be a gift to performers, as well as to their audiences. As we do not have either a "singing voice" or a "speaking voice," but one magnificent instrument that laughs, cries, whimpers, sighs, screams, calls out, and also speaks and sings, divisive labels give out the wrong information and create unnecessary barriers.

As I was teaching a voice class in an actor training program recently, a student said, "Until I got into this class, I thought there were two sets of muscles: one for speaking and one for singing." If you tell a class of actors that they have a speaking voice and a singing voice, most of them will tell you very quickly they don't have the singing one.

Commonly used divisive labels are both anatomically inaccurate and potentially damaging, as performers assume the tasks of singing and speaking have little connection, therefore attend to one, but not the other. So we have beautiful singers speaking in glottal fry and actors with glorious voices cringing in terror at the thought of singing.

Widening the lens further, voice is intimately connected to movement on many levels. Sound itself is movement, muscles move to create voice, as do fluids and air and virtually everything else in and around the body.

For years I've included yoga with voice (see *One Voice*, 82 – 93) in lessons and classes. And an initial reaction from many students—including master teachers of yoga—has been, "Wow, now it's complete." Far too often voice is cut off from physical activity. We've learned to "exercise," but also to "keep quiet."

Dance and voice have been learned separately by millions of performers who dance in silence and sing in stillness. Actors reconnected voice and movement at least 50 years ago, but singing was still a hothouse plant. Only now is voice beginning to enter the dance class, singing the acting class, and dancing with voice is a given in musical theatre.

Putting it all together in performance has been the focus of this book. John Robert Armstrong said, "It's all acting, and it's all one instrument" (Chapter 9). Bill Lett said, "When your body is your instrument, anything is possible with practice" (Chapter 2). And Francine Zerfas said, "[Movement] improved my experience of acting and helped me understand my voice beyond my training" (Chapter 3).

Reference

Melton, J, Tom, K. *One Voice: Integrating Singing and Theatre Voice Techniques*. 2nd ed. Long Grove, IL: Waveland, 2012.

Bibliography

Biel, A. *Trail Guide to the Body*. Boulder: Books of Discovery, 2001.

Callaghan, J. *Singing & Science: Body, Brain & Voice*. Oxford: Compton, 2014.

Chapman, J. *Singing and Teaching Singing: A Holistic Approach to Classical Voice*. San Diego: Plural, 2006.

Churcher, M. *Acting for Film: Truth 24 Times a Second*. London: Virgin, 2003.

Dayme, MB. *The Performer's Voice: Realizing Your Vocal Potential*. New York: WW Norton, 2005.

Greene Haas, J. *Dance Anatomy*. Champaign, IL: Human Kinetics, 2010.

Grieg, V. *Inside Ballet Technique: Separating Anatomical Fact from Fiction in the Ballet Class*. Heightstown, NJ: Dance Horizons, 1994.

Hawkins, C. "The Mechanics of Breathing as Applied to Different Vocal Tasks," *Communicating Voice*, Vol. 8 (1), August 2007, 8.

Hixon, TJ. *Respiratory Function in Singing: A Primer for Singers and Singing Teachers*. Tucson: Reddington Brown, 2006.

Homan, J. *Apollo's Angels: A History of Ballet*. New York: Random House, 2010.

Kayes, G. *Singing and the Actor*, 2nd ed. London: A & C Black (UK), New York: Routledge (USA and Canada), 2004.

Lederman, F.. "The Myth of Core Stability," CPDO Online Journal, June, 1007, 1 – 17, www.cpdo.net.

McCoy, S. *Your Voice: An Inside View*. Princeton: Inside View Press, 2004.

Macdonald, I, Rubin, JS, Blake, E, Hirani, S, Epstein, R. "An Investigation of Abdominal Muscle Recruitment for Sustained Phonation in 25 Healthy Singers," *Journal of Voice*, 26 (6), 2012, 815.e9 – e16.

Malde, M, Allen, MJ, Zeller, KA. *What Every Singer Needs to Know About the Body*. San Diego: Plural, 2009.

Melton, J. "Pilates and the Actor/Singer," *The Australian Voice*. Brisbane: Australian Voice Association, 2001, www.joanmelton.com/articles.

_____. *Singing in Musical Theatre: The Training of Singers and Actors*. New York: Allworth Press, 2007, www.joanmelton.com/singing-musical-theatre.

_____. *The Technical Core: Stage 1*, DVD. New York: Voice Theatre Solutions, 2009. Available by contacting joan.melton@joanmelton.com

_____. "Trainings Relate but Do Not Equate." VASTA Newsletter, fall 2009, www.joanmelton.com/articles.

Melton, J, Tom, K. *One Voice: Integrating Singing and Theatre Voice Techniques*, 2nd ed. Long Grove, IL: Waveland Press, 2012, www.joan-melton.com/books.

Morton, J. *The Authentic Performer: Wearing a Mask and the Effect on Health*. Oxford: Compton, 2015.

Rodenburg, P. *The Actor Speaks: Voice and the Performer.* London: Methuen Drama, 1997.

_____. *The Right to Speak.* London: Methuen Drama, 1992.

Saunders-Barton, M. *Bel Canto Can Belto: What About the Boys?* 2014. DVD tutorial and sequel to *Bel Canto Can Belto: Teaching Women to Sing Musical Theatre,* 2007. Available at www.belcantocanbelto.com.

Smith, S, Thyme, K. *Die Akzentmethod.* Vedback: The Danish Voice Institute, 1981.

Stone, R J & Stone, JA. *Atlas of Skeletal Muscles.* New York: McGraw-Hill, 2003.

Visible Body 3D Human Anatomy Atlas 2 App.

Watson, P, Hoit, J, Lansing, R, Hixon, T. "Abdominal Muscle Activity during Classical Singing," *Journal of Voice,* 3 (1), 1989, 24 – 31.

Zemlin, W. *Speech and Hearing Science,* 3rd ed. Boston: Allyn & Bacon, 1988.

Made in the USA
Middletown, DE
30 August 2015